RESTORATIVE
MOVING BEYOND PUNISHMENT
JUSTICE

by Harmon L. Wray

with Peggy Hutchison

Study Guide by Brenda Connelly

Photo/Art Credits: 44—Sarah Chowning • 81—John Coleman • 38—Bruce Cook • 71—John Goodman • 7, 33, 52—Helen Martin • 17—Bridget Sarabi • viii, 74, 77, 82—Peter Siegfried • 48—Pat Spaulding • UNICEF—59 • 63—David Wildman • 3—Harmon Wray • 49—John Cole Vodicka

Restorative Justice: Moving Beyond Punishment copyright © 2002 General Board of Global Ministries
A publication of the General Board of Global Ministries, The United Methodist Church

Cover design: John Havey

ISBN#1-890569-34-8

contents

P R E F A C E

"If one member suffers, all suffer together" (1 Corinthians 12:26).

Deep sorrow has touched all of our lives in the tragic events of September 11, 2001. Countless United Methodists have directly experienced the loss of family and friends. All of us grieve. Our prayers at this time of crisis give support to each other and to all who are suffering. We are so grateful for our supportive community in Christ.

Moreover, the most effective form of support that United Methodists can give is the kind that members are known for—ongoing commitment and action to make the world a better and safer place for everyone. We are committed to informed, prayerful action. Each year we study parts of the world of which we may only have heard before. Annually we seek deeper spiritual understanding not just to prepare us for the world's events, but to help shape them. Some years ago we studied Islam, and are now better equipped to advocate for tolerance instead of violence based on racial profiling.

As we watched the towers of the World Trade Center crumble, the shock and sense of powerlessness were overwhelming. But powerlessness is what we feel when we think we are alone and that everything rests on our shoulders. The future of our world rests on all of our shoulders together as we try to respond to God's call for peace and justice. We have a long history of overcoming powerlessness by working together, and by creating programs that give hope to the powerless and ease the burden of the oppressed. That spirit is calling us to come together now.

Joyce D. Sohl
Deputy General Secretary
Women's Division
General Board of Global Ministries

For many middle-class citizens of the United States, crime and punishment are not pleasant subjects, and for many in largely middle-class churches such as The United Methodist Church, they seem unrelated to our Christian faith. Or perhaps we see "prison ministry" as something a few Christians—say, state prison chaplains—are called to, over there on the margins of our consciousness.

If, on occasion, this other world should happen to intrude upon our lives and those of our families through criminal victimization, a drug problem, an arrest, jury duty, or being a witness to a crime, we handle it as quickly and easily as possible. Meanwhile, our comfortable neighborhoods, security systems, perhaps our concealed weapons (for self-defense only, of course), our lawyers, and our insurance policies keep us out of the line of fire.

There are others who live much closer to this ugly and terrifying world of crime, violence, courtrooms, jails, and prisons than anyone should have to. Sometimes they, too, live in middle-class neighborhoods and go to church with middle-class neighbors. Yet, they live—as victims or perpetrators—in a reality of domestic violence, substance abuse and addiction, juvenile delinquency, and crime even as they try desperately to navigate and function in a middle-class world of law and order, peace and quiet. More often, however, they live in a territory of suffering and poverty with little distance from the realities of crime and punishment in their daily lives. Every day is a struggle for economic and emotional survival, for dignity, and for respect, and they know little of the luxury of taking for granted these necessary elements of human life.

Unfortunately, in the United Methodist Church there is seldom much overt attention to, or conversation about, the undeniable fact of class privilege. Many of us believe that we in North America are a classless society, a land of equal opportunity. The reality is very different. Along with gender, matters of race and class are so intertwined in our lives that it is almost impossible to sort them out when we try to analyze a particular problem—for instance, crime and punishment. Yet it is important that we try. If our different histories and perspectives along the lines of gender, class, and race affect how we experience and understand the realities of crime and punishment, so does our church experience. How we read and understand the Bible, how we experience the Holy Spirit, how we know Jesus, how we imagine and think of God—all these determine in large part how we think, feel, and behave, personally and as a society, with respect to crime and the justice system.

A few moments' reflection will help us see that crime and punishment are central to the Bible and our faith. We need read no further than Genesis 4, before we are confronted by Cain's murder of Abel, and God's response of both exile and protection from human vengeance. A few chapters later we find the story of Jacob and Esau, a relationship fraught with envy, guilt, antagonism, and fear from the moment they emerged from their mother's womb. It is a story that finally culminates in reconciliation, but only after many years of bitterness. Next is the rape of Leah and Jacob's daughter Dinah, and the avenging of Dinah by her brothers. Soon we are with the story of Joseph, sold into slavery by his brothers and later imprisoned by his master, but ultimately reconciled to his brothers years later. And the stories continue throughout the Hebrew Scriptures.

Thematically speaking, both retribution and restoration, both harshness and healing, seem to be major, intertwined factors in the Hebrew understanding of justice. On the one hand, we find the *lex talionis* (an eye for an eye and a tooth or a tooth)—which appears three times in the Hebrew Scriptures—and a compilation of at least twenty-three crimes carrying the death penalty. On the other hand is the recognition that the *lex talionis* was intended more as a limit and restraint against excessive vengeance than as a mandate to seek revenge. And the rich language of *shalom*—a word used 350 times in the Bible—points to God's desire for God's children to live in right relationship, which today we might call peace with justice.

When we move on to the New Testament, very quickly we have Herod's genocide of male infants in and near Bethlehem. Then comes John the Baptizer—imprisoned and executed. Jesus' relationship to Jewish law is a major thread running through the gospels and the rest of the New Testament. Speaking technically and literally, Jesus' life can be characterized as that of a criminal—a lawbreaker. Eventually, of course, he was arrested, imprisoned, tried, convicted, condemned, and executed by the Roman legal system, with the full support of the political and religious establishments of his time and place, and with the support of public opinion. Many books in the New Testament were written from prison, and many of Jesus' early followers, including Stephen and most of the apostles, were also executed.

The history of the Christian church's teaching and behavior concerning issues of crime and justice is no cause for celebration. After an initial three centuries or so of relative fidelity to the nonviolent, healing emphasis of Jesus, and a corresponding distancing from the violence and retributive ways of the state, things changed with the fourth-century conversion of Roman emperor Constantine. The church's stance toward the state began to shift from one of tension to one of accommodation. Since then, with few exceptions, the church has shifted to a rigid, violent, punitive, retributive, state-dominated style of justice, away from a flexible, nonviolent, reparative, community-based approach.

The history of the post-Constantinian, Catholic, and Reformation churches throughout and after the Middle Ages was a turning away from a norm of what historian Howard Zehr calls community justice—characterized by decentralized, victim-centered, and negotiated processes and by reparative sanctions—to a dominant model of state justice, far more hierarchical, externally imposed, and punishment-oriented.

The eighteenth-century Enlightenment and the French Revolution consolidated this legal revolution with a new legitimization of state power. Now the state had a monopoly on justice, on legitimate violence, and on power, and it was in a position to use this monopoly to exercise social control over internal political threats through public and decisive dramatization of its dominance.

The almost simultaneous births of the modern prison (Philadelphia's Walnut Street Jail in 1790) and of the justice system of the United States, and their subsequent rapid growth, represent perhaps the culmination of this long history of justice understood as punishment, and the decline of a more biblical form of community justice.

The powerful fundamentalist strain in our faith tradition has helped to shape both our national proclivity to choose violence to "resolve" conflict and the image of God as harshly punitive, which have fostered in our culture both violent crime and retributive responses to crime. Our attempts to biblically justify patriarchy and the subjugation of women have led to an epidemic of domestic violence, efforts to use the criminal law to deny reproductive choice to women, and, currently, an unprecedented rise in the incarceration of women.

Our pietistic moralism has helped shape the mentality that illegal drug users should be punished much more severely than tycoons who pollute the air breathed by millions of human beings. Our moral hypocrisy has helped us turn a blind eye to the blatant discrepancy between how our society treats the marijuana smoker as compared with those who consume alcohol and tobacco. Our theologically distorted racism and its legacies of genocide against aboriginal peoples, enslavement of Africans, and racial segregation of African Americans and other people of color, have laid the groundwork for the vastly disproportionate number of our citizens who live in poverty; for the street crime that bedevils their communities; and for the massive racism evident in all stages of our criminal justice system.

This study book is an effort to help United Methodists understand and then transform the harsh and forbidding reality of crime, substance abuse, violence, and a court and prison system with unprecedented power. At the same time, it is an invitation to discipleship, offering a way to walk with Jesus within a community of faith and witness dedicated to his vision of ministry with the victims (Luke 10:25-37), hospitable presence with those in prison (Matthew 25:31-46), and liberty to the captives (Isaiah 61:1-2 and Luke 4:16-30).

"The criminal justice system does not protect us from the gravest threats to life, limb, or possessions. Its definitions of crime are not simply a reflection of the objective dangers that threaten us."

—Jeffrey Reiman

1

THE SYSTEM NOBODY LIKES:
A CRITICAL ANALYSIS OF THE CRIMINAL JUSTICE SYSTEM

In the year 2000, the prison population in the United States increased for the twenty-eighth consecutive year. What we euphemistically call the "corrections" system, has become one of the fastest-growing budget items in almost every state of the union. The United States imprisons a higher percentage of its people than any other nation in the world—702 per 100,000 as of July 2001, according to the International Center for Prison Studies. Russia, with 635 per 100,000, was second. The United States, with 7 percent of the world's population, has 25 percent of the world's prisoners. And, with less than 25 percent of China's population, the United States imprisons 500,000

people more than do the Chinese.

The United States also has the longest sentences of any country in the world. However, a recent analysis attributes the rise in incarceration rates to an increase in time served in prison, rather than to actual sentencing. Furthermore, in recent years fourteen states and the federal prison system have eliminated parole, and many others have increased the rate of parole and probation revocations, thus driving up even further the growing rate of imprisonment.

State-by-state breakdowns of these statistics show that the eight jurisdictions with the highest rates of incarceration in the year 2000 are all southern (Alabama, Georgia, Louisiana, Mississippi, Oklahoma, South Carolina, Texas—and the District of Columbia). However, the top six states showing the greatest increases in rates of imprisonment since 1980 are all northern and western (California, Connecticut, Idaho, New Hampshire, New Jersey, North Dakota). New Jersey, at 143 percent of capacity, has the most crowded prison system in the country, followed closely by Illinois and Wisconsin.

Who are all these prisoners? The smallest group by far—approximately 1 percent—consists of white-collar, corporate criminals. Of the 1.14 million in state prisons in 1998, approximately 135,000 were murderers, 100,000 sex offenders, and 160,000 armed robbers—crimes that fit the stereotype of violent predators. Interestingly, those numbers added up to roughly 35 percent of all prisoners. Most of the others were there for offenses related to property, public order, and drugs.

The European Union's total prison population (to provide some global perspective) is one-third the size of the United States' nonviolent prisoner population alone. And Europe's overall population is 25 percent larger than that of the United States. An even more striking contrast: The entire prison population of India, a country with roughly four times our population, is only one-fifth of the United States' nonviolent prison and jail population of 1.2 million.

The U.S. federal prison population is even more weighted toward nonviolent offenders. Of the 109,000 federal prisoners in 1998, only 11 percent were there for violent offenses; 20 percent for public order offenses; 9 percent for property crimes; and an astonishing 60 percent for drug offenses. Indeed, criminal justice experts who have studied the recent burgeoning of incarceration rates in the United States have focused on the drug war as the primary cause of this unprecedented development.

Today in the United States, ten times as many people—450,000—are in jails and prisons for drug offenses than in 1980. The percentage of the total jail and prison population represented by drug offenders jumped from 6 percent to 22 percent during this same period. Although the federal prison system has the most disproportionate number of nonviolent drug offenders, some states also have high proportions. The top ten are spread through all regions of the country: Arizona, California, Delaware, Illinois, New Jersey, New York, Oklahoma, South Carolina, Tennessee, Utah.

If our government's war on illegal drugs is responsible for much of the sharp rise in incarceration over the last two decades, another important factor is race. On any given day, one-third of the nation's black males in their twenties are under the control of the criminal justice system—in prison or jail, on probation or parole. (Information is based on research of The Sentencing Project, Washington, D.C.) The Justice Department recently estimated that in the year 2000, 12 percent of black males in their twenties and early thirties were in prison or jail. (Jails, usually housing both pre-trial defendants and convicts serving time, are operated by county governments. Prisons, where felony convicts are housed, are operated by states and by the federal government.)

If current trends continue, three out of every ten black males born today can expect to do time in jail or prison, compared to 16 percent of Hispanic males and 4 percent of white males. Today's U.S. prison population is 49 percent black and 18 percent Hispanic. At the end of the administration of Bill Clinton—the man the Nobel Prize-winning writer Toni Morrison once referred to as "our first black president"—the African-American incarceration rate was 3,620 per 100,000. When Native Americans and Asian Americans are factored in as well, the states with the greatest disparity in incarceration rates for whites vs. people of color are all northeastern and midwestern: Connecticut, Illinois, Maryland, Minnesota, New Jersey, New York, Ohio, Pennsylvania, Wisconsin—and the District of Columbia. Of the 1.4 million state prisoners in 1998, approximately 135,000 were murderers; 100,000 were sex offenders, and 160,000 were armed robbers—crimes that fit the stereotype of violent predators, adding up to roughly 35 percent of all prisoners. Most of the rest were there for property offenses, public order offenses, and drug offenses.

If we look at African American incarceration figures, it becomes clear that the much-ballyhooed war on drugs is, in reality, a selective war on young, poor, black males from the inner cities. While African Americans constitute about 15 percent of regular illegal drug users in this country (close to their 13 percent of the national population), they make up 35 percent of those arrested for illegal drug possession; 55 percent of drug convictions; and 74 percent of those incarcerated for drug possession. It becomes clear that—intentional or not—racism plays a significant role in each of the following stages of the criminal justice process: arrest, conviction, and sentencing. The cumulative effect is devastating.

When coupled with laws in most states that do not grant the vote to convicted felons (an estimated four million people, 1.4 million of whom have completed their terms are affected), 13 percent of adult black men in the United States are unable to vote. Rev. Jesse Jackson has put it well: "The gains of the civil rights movement are thus being rolled back by the march of the prison industrial complex." It is surely no accident that many of the thirteen states that disenfranchise felons for life were part of the old Confederacy. Thirty-one percent of black men in Alabama and Florida are permanently unable to vote because of a felony conviction. This fact, of course, had a decisive impact on the outcome of the 2000 presidential election.

For a truly startling perspective on the number of imprisoned black men in the United States, consider this: In 1993, during the apartheid regime in South Africa—a nation internationally condemned as the most racist society on earth—the incarceration rate for black men was 851 per 100,000. During the last year of Clinton's presidency, the incarceration rate for black men was 7,119 per 100,000—more than eight times the South African rate seven years earlier.

Although in our society males are much more likely to be imprisoned than females, there have been significant changes. The incarceration rate of adult males has quadrupled in the past two decades; that for adult females has quintupled. Of the 93,000 women locked up in state and federal prisons in 1997, 34.4 percent had a drug charge as their most serious offense. Another 71,000 women were serving short sentences or awaiting trial in local jails. The majority of both groups was either African American or Latina.

In 1999 almost half of these women told Department of Justice officials that they had been physically or sexually abused before their imprisonment, compared with 10 percent of male prisoners. While two-thirds of women on probation are white, two-thirds of those incarcerated are people of color. Women in prison are more likely than men to be illegal drug users and less likely to be drinkers. Researchers agree that women in prison are often battered and poorly educated. Incarcerated women themselves report a higher rate of mental illness than do male prisoners.

Other important factors in analyzing our prison population are educational level and health. Almost two-thirds of United States prisoners are high school dropouts; 70 percent are functionally illiterate. In many prisons there are extremely high rates of HIV/AIDS (an estimated 47,000 nationally), hepatitis C (an estimated 41 percent in California prisons), and tuberculosis (rates as high as 25 percent in some prisons). Even with such alarming percentages, prison officials are notoriously resistant to the monitoring of illness levels and the provision of health care in their institutions.

However, the bleakest realm for imprisoned populations may be that of mental health. Over the last several decades, our society's deinstitutionalization policies—the downsizing or closing of residential mental health hospitals—and its failure to develop a strong, well-funded network of small, community-based mental health centers has been disastrous. It has led to a massive increase in homelessness, as well as the dumping of many

mentally ill persons into the lap of a criminal justice system that is ill-prepared to deal with them humanely or effectively.

In 1999, based on reports by prisoners in the mid-90s, the Department of Justice announced that an estimated 284,000 mentally ill prisoners were being held in jails and prisons. Only 60 percent reported that they had received any form of treatment during their time in prison. A study completed in the year 2000 indicates that only 70 percent of state prisons routinely screen prisoners for mental illness.

It is important to remember that, like everyone, prisoners and other criminal offenders are not isolated individuals who can be punished without considering anyone else. There are, first of all, their victims—whose relationship with them is very important for criminal justice purposes—but also parents, siblings, and children (who may also be their victims). Prisoners' families are so profoundly and so negatively affected by the consequences of the crime and the punishment that one might well call them secondary victims. The indirect consequences for the rest of the society are also profound.

Experts estimate that more than 10 million children in the United States have experienced the imprisonment of a parent. One prison support worker calls it the largest separation of families since slavery. Nearly half of imprisoned parents are black; 20 percent are Hispanic. Overall, black children are nine times as likely as white children to have a parent in prison. For Hispanic children the figure is three times. In 1997, 1.5 million children in the United States had at least one parent in prison; in 1991 the figure was fewer than a million.

Ninety percent of imprisoned fathers reported that at least one child was in the care of the mother, but only 28 percent of imprisoned mothers said that one of their children was living with the father. Average sentences being served by these parents ranged from 10 to 12 years in state and federal prisons. Forty percent of the fathers and 60 percent of the mothers in state prisons reported some form of weekly contact with their children, but more than half said they had never had a visit from their children. Less than half of imprisoned parents said they had lived with their children before their incarceration.

Studies show that children of parents in prison, most already suffering from the effects of high poverty rates,

PATCH and MATCH

Prison PATCH (Parents And Their Children)

PATCH of Chillicothe, Missouri, provides regular visitation between incarcerated mothers and their children in a homelike visiting center under PATCH supervision, but within prison walls. Such visits are attempts to keep the lines of communication open between mothers and their children.

PATCH's goal is to reunite families that have been separated by incarceration, and to break intergenerational patterns of violence and criminal behavior by sending mothers back home to their children, prepared to be better parents.

PATCH expects to see a reduction in the recidivism of incarcerated women; to track children who have been clients of PATCH; and to see more children complete high school, stay crime-free, and become productive members of their communities.

Prison MATCH

(Mothers And Their Children)

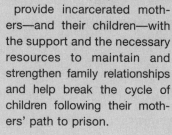

Prison MATCH in North Carolina was modeled after Prison PATCH, whose purpose is to provide incarcerated mothers—and their children—with the support and the necessary resources to maintain and strengthen family relationships and help break the cycle of children following their mothers' path to prison.

Both PATCH and MATCH provide in-depth parenting classes, and arrange transportation for children to come to the centers to visit their incarcerated moms.

Both of these ministries have had major support from United Methodist Women—financial and in the form of volunteers—in implementing and continuing their programs. PATCH, which began twenty years ago, and MATCH, which started ten years ago, continue to be viable today. (Prison PATCH was modeled after Prison MATCH in the Federal Correctional Institution at Pleasanton, California; Prison MATCH, North Carolina, was modeled after Prison PATCH.)

Comments from mothers who recently received visits from their children in the PATCH Center

■ Sonya* had visits with her daughter over a period of several days. The visits were "great". It seems that she and her daughter have stayed bonded "real well," although many of their contacts have just been phone calls and pictures.

■ Calita* recently had a visit with her son, and describes him as a "deep thinker." She said, "I want my child to be a child," and knows that one never regains one's childhood once those years are over.

* not real name

substance abuse by their parents, as well as neglect and abuse by their parents or others, are at greater risk than other children of almost every bad experience imaginable: depression, acting out, poor academic performance, early pregnancy, substance abuse, post-traumatic stress disorder, shame, self-loathing, survivor guilt, flashbacks, and problems with sleep and concentration. Here, again, the prison industry guarantees future business for itself. According to the Center for Children of Incarcerated Parents, half the male children of prisoners will engage in criminal activity and enter the juvenile justice system before they are eighteen. Another researcher reports that children of prisoners are five times more likely than others to end up in prison themselves.

In analyzing the current state of the criminal justice system, it is crucial to think about the future of prisoners after their release, since they will return to large numbers of communities throughout the country. It is fair to say that most of them will not be ready to return to society outside prison walls. Prisoners serve longer sentences than ever, which has the destabilizing effect of loosening their ties with the world outside prison—family, friends, employers, etc. It also means that their job skills, if any, are likely to have deteriorated. In addition, meaningful job training and educational programs, drug treatment, and rehabilitation have declined significantly. Many prisoners are released directly to the street with no parole supervision or support system.

Because of the huge rise in incarceration over the past three decades, the sheer number of prisoners released each year has also risen sharply. It is projected that more than 600,000 were released in 2001. Based on previous studies of recidivism (repeat arrest and/or incarceration), close to two-thirds will be rearrested on felony or serious misdemeanor charges within three years. Over 40 percent of those rearrested will be sent back to prison.

We turn now to the juvenile justice system. Of the 120,000 young people currently imprisoned in the United States, an estimated 50 to 75 percent have a diagnosable mental disorder, and 15 to 20 percent suffer from severe mental illness. These numbers appear to be on the increase. Among girls in the system, more than 75 percent have been sexually abused.

Although children of color constitute just one-third of the nation's youth population, they make up two-thirds of all youth locked up in local and state facilities. Black youthful offenders without previous records are six times more likely to go to prison than white youth without previous records. This constitutes seriously disproportionate imprisonment of minorities. Imprisoned black youth are less likely than whites to receive mental health treatment.

In an ominous trend that threatens to eviscerate this country's historic and distinctive juvenile justice system, with its priority on "the best interests of the child," all fifty states now have provisions for juveniles to be tried as adults. Seven thousand children each year are sent to adult prisons. In practice, these provisions have a disproportionate impact on minority young people: African American youth are responsible for fewer than half of all juvenile felony cases, but they account for two-thirds of cases transferred from the juvenile to the adult criminal court system.

These disturbing trends were fueled in 1996

by the terrifying and widely publicized warnings of John DiIulio (later to become President George W. Bush's director of faith-based and community initiatives) of the imminent invasion of huge numbers of "super-predators": young criminals who would lay waste U.S. communities. The predicted storm never materialized. In fact, the trend in juvenile violent crime has been sharply in the opposite direction. But the damage had been done, and it persists. In 1998, 62 percent of the adults surveyed believed that youth crime was increasing. This despite the facts:

- Between 1993 and 1999, the homicide arrest rate for juveniles plunged 68 percent to its lowest level since 1966. The rate for white perpetrators fell more than 50 percent; the rate for blacks fell an astounding 72 percent.

- Between 1993 and 1999, the arrest rate of juveniles for the four major violent crimes taken together—murder, rape, robbery, and aggravated assault—dropped 36 percent.

- Between 1997 and 1999, juvenile drug abuse violations, and curfew and loitering violations, dropped 17 percent and 13 percent, respectively.

- In 1999, drug and alcohol use among juveniles, while high, remained unchanged from the previous year, and cigarette use declined.

Not only is juvenile crime diminishing sharply, but the currently favored solutions for the problem are, if anything, counterproductive. A federally commissioned report from 2001 suggests that hard-line programs—such as "Scared Straight" or juvenile boot camp—either have no effect or actually increase juvenile delinquency, and that imprisonment seems to have only nega-

tive effects on the prevalence of juvenile crime. According to the report, Massachusetts and Missouri, which treat most juvenile offenders in community-based alternative programs, are on the right track in terms of both effectiveness and cost. Another recent study found that youth who had been prosecuted in criminal court were rearrested within two years of their release at a rate more than 50 percent higher than those who had been kept in the juvenile court system.

A special high-profile category of youth crime is school violence. While such violence is profoundly tragic, as well as terrifying, the hype is far greater than the reality, as one will find when examining the numbers. Although 70 percent of United States residents are afraid that a school shooting might happen in their community, a child has a one-in-2-million chance of being killed in school. In 1997-1998, of the 3000 children who were murdered or who killed themselves, only 42—or 1.4 percent—died at school. There has been a steady decline in violent school crime since 1992. In fact, home is by far the most dangerous place for children—worse than the street, and far worse than school.

A striking feature of the statistical picture is that this rapid rise in the rate of imprisonment has coincided with a consistently downward slide in the crime rate, as measured both by police and household reports of victimization. The United States still has one of the highest rates of violent crime in the world, largely because of the ease with which we can obtain increasingly lethal guns and ammunition, but it is falling, and our other crime statistics are comparable with similar nations.

The annual National Crime Victimization

Survey (NCVS), which gathers and analyzes data in response to questions asked of a scientific sample of households, provides a more accurate measure of true crime rates than do the annual FBI Uniform Crime Reports. The FBI reports measure only those crimes reported to police (44 percent of violent crimes and 34 percent of property crimes in 1999, with rape as the least reported serious crime, at only 28 percent). In 1999, by NCVS measures, U.S. residents over the age of 12 were victimized by 21.2 million property crimes (household burglary, car theft, and theft)—198 per 1,000 households—and 7.4 million violent crimes (murder, rape, sexual assault, robbery, aggravated assault, and simple assault)—33 per 1,000 households.

Although the raw numbers are staggering, between 1993 and 1999 rates of violent crime fell 34 percent and those of property fell 38 percent. It is likely that this recent decline in the crime rate has been primarily the result of demographic trends; a stronger economy in the 1990s; more stringent gun control laws; better policing; and changes in the crack-cocaine trade. Most criminologists believe that the decline has little to do with rapidly increasing incarceration rates, which have been pervasive in most states and in the federal system since about 1970, especially in the 1980s and 1990s. Indeed, our national crime rate, despite a steady fall, still remains higher than it was when we locked up one-sixth the number of people we do now, and it is clear that trends in current crime rates and trends in rates of imprisonment do not correlate.

The decline in the crime rate has also been accompanied by a sharp increase in mainstream media coverage of street crime—especially violent street crime. As the homicide rate in the United States dropped 50 percent between 1990 and 1998, the three major television networks' coverage of homicide stories rose almost 400 percent. It seems that we are imprisoning and executing people not in response to a crime wave, but in reaction to political and media-driven fear of crime. Like the war on drugs, an "if it bleeds, it leads" media policy of exaggerated coverage of violent crime and law enforcement is a deliberate choice, in this case driven by considerations of profit.

Joe Hallinan, reporter for the *Wall Street Journal* and author of *Going Up the River: Travels in a Prison Nation*, rightly sees the prison boom as the result of a deadly combination of financial self-interest, political corruption, and public fear of crime. "I gradually began to see it as parallel to the communist scare of the 1950s," Hallinan recalls. "Back then, the generalized fear bred a huge military arsenal. Now it breeds prisons." Quite apart from the human and spiritual price, the financial cost of this national binge of locking people up in cages is huge. Prison construction is estimated at $50,000 per prisoner, and the average cost of one year in state prison for one adult is $23,000. (Alternative sanctions such as drug and alcohol treatment and intensive supervision during probation cost $2,500 and $6,000 respectively for the same period, according to the National Committee on Community Corrections.) The annual figure for imprisoning a juvenile is even higher: $35,000 (compared to $7,000 for a year of public school). Estimates of the total annual cost of the prison system throughout the United

States range from $40 billion to $50 billion, but the most recent ones put it at approximately $45 billion, as compared with $7 million in 1980.

Costs of the many other parts of the criminal justice system—police, courts, parole, etc.— drive the overall figures much higher. Meanwhile, gated communities, home security systems, private guns, private business and residential security personnel, and the like, consume many more millions. Finally, public assistance for families of the imprisoned and foster care for their children vastly increase the total costs related to imprisoning millions of people.

Most citizens of the United States—many of them people of faith—seem to assume that the answer to crime is punishment. Most do not recognize that excessive punishment may be part of the problem rather than part of the solution. Another often ignored reality is that corporate and white-collar crime—as opposed to street crime— is seldom punished by imprisonment, though every year the loss to corporate crime of human life, health, and personal property vastly exceeds the loss to crimes committed by the poor, who lack access to the tools with which to commit these more sophisticated forms of crime.

According to Ralph Nader in a speech at Vanderbilt University, all street crimes resulting in criminal homicide number about 15,500 annually, while corporate and white collar crimes result in the following: an estimated 58,000 deaths resulting from workplace-induced disease (usually from toxic poisons) or injury (usually caused by unsafe working conditions); approximately 80,000 preventable deaths per year from medical incompetence in hospitals alone; 400,000 preventable

tobacco-related deaths per year; 65,000 preventable deaths resulting from air pollution; an estimated 100,000 deaths a year as a result of doctors' or pharmacists' mistakes in prescription medications. No wonder that during the 2000 presidential campaign, when asked his position on the death penalty, Nader replied that he had been opposed to it since he learned in law school how it really worked, but that he did make one exception: he supports the death penalty for "antisocial corporations."

In his book *The Rich Get Richer and the Poor Get Prison* (6th edition, Allyn & Bacon: Needham Heights, MA, 2001), Jeffrey Reiman develops a similar argument, arriving at more conservative (but still devastating) figures for corporate deaths as compared with official criminal homicides. He also calculates dollar and property loss, as well as personal injury and permanent illness figures. His conclusions are dramatic:

> The criminal justice system does not protect us from the gravest threats to life, limb, or possessions. Its definitions of crime are not simply a reflection of the objective dangers that threaten us. The workplace, the medical profession, the air we breathe, and the poverty we refuse to rectify lead to far more human suffering, far more death and disability, and take far more dollars from our pockets than the murders, aggravated assaults, and thefts reported annually by the FBI. What is more, this human suffering is preventable.

Another piece of this grim social landscape is the convergence of corporate greed and political cynicism in the privatization of prisons. Since the founding of the Corrections Corporation of America in 1983, the specter of private, for-profit prisons has been stalking the land, particularly across the Sunbelt. This is no accident. These states have historically higher rates of crime, punishment by incarceration, and violence. They also tend to be "right-to-work" states with weak labor movements. Since organized labor has been the principal force of effective opposition to private, for-profit prisons, it follows that the prison firms would target these states for growth. As of mid-year 2001, the number of private prison beds in the United States had increased seven-fold in nine years.

The effort to privatize prisons is part of a much larger and growing so-called prison industrial complex (PIC), which rivals the earlier military industrial complex in demonstrating how corporate greed drives public policy. Basically, the PIC notion refers to the way in which corporate interests and the profit motive—not concerns of public safety, equal justice, rehabilitation, or restitution to victims—are increasingly determining criminal justice policy in this country. As citizens and taxpayers, we must educate ourselves about the PIC, that is, about private prisons and how the criminal justice system is being used as a force for racism, social control, patriarchy, and repression of dissent, and as a dumping ground for human beings regarded by the dominant sectors of society as toxic waste.

It is instructive to compare the prison industrial complex with the military industrial complex, a concept first articulated in 1960 by former President Dwight D. Eisenhower in his farewell address. Eisenhower expressed concern that the profit motive of military corporate contractors was having increasing influence on our foreign policy. Later commentators cited the "revolving door" through which certain persons traveled between Pentagon jobs and jobs as executives and consultants for such corporations. Furthermore, there were—and are—the ways in which such individuals and corporations influence congressional votes and executive branch decisions through lobbyists and contributions to political campaigns.

Today, journalists and critics of the U.S. prison system point to the political influence of powerful organizations with a vested interest in expanding incarceration. A partial list would include the following: private prison companies; prison food service and health care companies; prison construction and architecture firms; long-distance telephone companies; prisoner guards' unions; the National Rifle Association; and makers of surveillance equipment, prison cell hardware, and weapons (including some former military contractors seeking new markets after the demise of the Cold War).

The influence of the prison system is not theoretical, but can dominate a small town. In "An American Seduction: Portrait of a Prison Town," (*Verdict*, magazine of the National Coalition of Concerned Legal Professionals, vol. 7, no. 2, April 2001), Joelle Fraser writes poignantly of the changes in her California home town, Susanville, since it became dominated by two prisons. She provides examples of "an industry for whom the raw material is the systematic incapacitation of hostile, despairing human beings." She speaks of "the constant talk of prison scandals and violence" and "the clear division between locals and prison employees and inmate families." She takes note of the sharp increase in traffic, prices, juvenile delinquency, gangs, divorce, domestic violence, the drug trade, and alcoholism—most of the trouble deriving from the correctional officers' families rather than those of the prisoners. In conclusion, Fraser raises "an underlying question: [C]an any economy based on human punishment be good in the end?" Her answer is not a happy one: "[T]he profound truth of a prison town is that its future is sentenced as surely as the inmates'. Most of the inmates, though, can leave when their time is done, but the town will never leave the prison. Or more precisely: the prison will never leave this town. No escape."

Marc Mauer of The Sentencing Project is a well-known researcher, writer, and advocate for alternatives to prison. Tracy Huling is an independent filmmaker and activist whose "Yes, in My Backyard" is the portrait of an upstate New York prison town no doubt much like Susanville, California. During the 2000 census, they wrote a newspaper piece about the poor African American and Hispanic inner-city neighborhoods from which most prisoners come, as well as the economically struggling but middle-class, primarily white rural areas to which they go when they are imprisoned. The authors note that the census, the results of which form the basis of federal and state legislative reapportionment and government funding, count prisoners as residing where they are incarcerated rather than where they come from. This is, in effect, a redistribution of political power and public wealth from impoverished communities to ones far from wealthy, but far more affluent.

Noting, for example, that in New York state 89 percent of prisoners are housed in rural areas, and 75 percent of the state's prisoners come from just seven New York City neighborhoods, they draw the obvious conclusion: "Thus, the urban communities hit hardest by both crime and criminal justice policies are now similarly disadvantaged by losing funding and political influence through the reapportionment process." Huling and Mauer's bottom line is this: "Both urban and rural communities face serious economic problems. But the elaborate shell game of ever-increasing incarceration distracts us from pursuing more constructive economic development while failing to address the underlying poverty and substance abuse that contribute so significantly to crime" ("Locked Up in the Census Count," *Chicago Tribune*, March 29, 2000).

The one person who has done more than anyone else to lift up the phenomenon of the prison industrial complex is author and activist Angela Davis of the University of California at Santa Cruz. In a 1998 essay, "Critical Resistance: Beyond the Prison Industrial Complex," Davis articulates the peculiar blend of racism, hatred of the poor, and magical thinking that characterizes the dominant public and private ethos at this stage of our history:

> Imprisonment has become the response of first resort to far too many of the social problems that burden people who are ensconced in poverty. These problems are often veiled by being conveniently grouped together under the category "crime" and by the automatic attribution of criminal behavior to people of color.

Homelessness, unemployment, drug addiction, mental illness, and illiteracy are only a few of the problems that disappear from public view when the human beings contending with them are relegated to cages.

Prisons thus perform a feat of magic. Or rather the people who continually vote in new prison bonds and tacitly assent to a proliferating network of prisons and jails have been tricked into believing in the magic of imprisonment. But prisons do not disappear problems, they disappear human beings. And the practice of disappearing vast numbers of people from poor, immigrant, and racially marginalized communities has literally become big business. . . .

The dividends that accrue from investment in the prison industry, like those that accrue from investment in weapons production, only amount to social destruction.

We have said much about criminal offenders and their families who suffer from the prison industrial complex, and of the interlocking triumvirate of special interests that benefit from it—corporations, mainstream media groups, and politicians. But what about the victims? How do victims of crime fit into this picture? Why have we not written about them?

Ah, but that is precisely the point. We have been describing and analyzing the justice system as it truly is, not as it pretends to be. The retributive, adversarial criminal justice system under which we operate—while making a pretense of making victims feel better by exacting revenge on their behalf and by giving them "closure"—is not set up to benefit the victims any more than it is to help offenders. Although the situation varies by location, for the most part crime victims are either marginalized and expected to be passive, or manipulated and exploited as good witnesses or good public relations tools for the political agenda of police and prosecutors. They are discouraged from any openness or connection with the designated offender, and they are discouraged from talking with the defense lawyers.

The adversary system discourages defendants from being active and outspoken. It dissuades them from expressing remorse or meeting with the victim. Often it creates in the defendant the feeling that he/she is the real victim, which is altogether accurate in a minority of cases, but feeds into many offenders' tendency to deny the seriousness of the harm they have done their victims. Little wonder that many in both groups—victims and criminal defendants alike—feel that the court process is not about them, but, rather, that it is run for the convenience and the interests of lawyers and judges. Victims and criminal defendants alike often feel like pawns on the chessboard, manipulated and moved around by those who know (because they wrote) the rules and are completely in charge.

So let us talk, if only briefly, about the victims (in this discussion not the victims of corporate, medical, and environmental harm). Strikingly, in 1999, 54 percent of all violent crime victims knew the perpetrator—as acquaintance, friend, relative, or intimate. This is true of almost 70 percent of rape or sexual assault victims. As we examine the demographics by economic class, generally the higher one's income, the lower one's chance of being the victim of violent crime. The gap between the middle to upper classes and the lowest classes is huge. For property crime, the rates of victimization tend to be more evenly spread out in terms of victims' income.

In 1999, males were victims of violent crime at a rate 28 percent greater than females, but females were the victims of rape and sexual assault at a rate 7.5 times greater than that of males.

It is important to note here that the NCVS does not include crimes committed in adult and juvenile prisons; an estimated 240,000 men are raped in prison annually, compared to 141,000 rapes of women in the "free" world in 1999. As of this writing, I know of no estimate of rapes of women in prison. Since our patriarchal culture often tends to blame female victims of male crimes, it is likely that male-on-female rape, sexual assault, and domestic violence are under-reported. Males are more likely to victimize females violently than vice versa. Strikingly, the age group most likely to be victimized by violent crime is 12 to 24.

Violent crime victimization rates for Hispanics and non-Hispanics in 1999 were very similar. Blacks, however, were victimized by violent crimes at rates higher than whites and than other races considered together. Native Americans, while numerically a small group, were victims of violent crime at much higher rates than all other races during the period 1993-1998. Blacks were also more likely in 1999 to be the victims of property crimes. For both violent and property crimes, residents of western states and of cities were more likely to be victimized than those in other regions or in suburban or rural areas.

Looking specifically at murder, based on the FBI Uniform Crime Reports, males account for three-quarters of murder victims; blacks account for half of murder victims; and one in eight of those murdered are younger than eighteen years of age. Firearms are used in approximately 70 percent of homicides, and large cities experience homicide at higher rates that do smaller cities and rural areas. Homicide rates are highest in the south and lowest in the northeastern states.

Since the predominant stereotype of a crime victim is a white, middle-class, elderly woman, it is striking that in reality the most typical victim of a "street crime" or "blue-collar crime" is a young, poor, black male. That this is startling information to many older, affluent, white persons is in itself both a scandal and a revelation.

This retributive system has been described as a "kind of trail 'em, nail 'em, jail 'em mentality." Restorative justice asks,"Who has been hurt? What are their needs? Whose obligation is it to meet their needs?"

2

IMAGINING AN ALTERNATIVE SYSTEM: RESTORATIVE JUSTICE

Sometimes it seems that everywhere in the world—our homes, our streets, the halls of government, even our religious institutions—people are continually at each other's throats, wanting what the other has. Individually and collectively, we always seem to want more—of something. We are stressed out, we are hostile, and too many of us are armed. Greed and violence, somehow rooted in fear and insecurity, seem always around us and, if we are honest, within us. Sometimes we experience these traits and emotions as controllable impulses. At other times, however, violence assumes the form of threats or intimidation used to seek or maintain disproportionate wealth or power over others. Or it erupts—sometimes cold and impersonal, sometimes hot and highly charged—threatening to destroy both violated and violator. Conflict, be it internal or external, on the surface or barely hidden, seems to define our lives.

To guard against these impulses we have established dogmatic theologies, moral codes, civil and criminal laws, courts, police, prisons, and treaties and protocols among nations. Yet, too often these "powers and principalities," as the Bible calls them, have assumed characteristics of the very evils they were meant to counter. Our criminal justice system's reliance on punishment, for example, is not the solution to crime, but a big part of the problem. Our institutional greed and violence are rooted in the same fear, anxiety, pride, and desire for revenge that undergird those realities in our personal lives.

There is, however, hope. Restorative justice is a wide-ranging movement that seeks to transform existing systems for dealing with interpersonal and intergroup conflict. Rooted in older, indigenous, tribal traditions of community justice, and in the biblical traditions of *shalom*, Jubilee economics, and the Sermon on the Mount, restorative justice refocuses our gaze and reshapes the questions and assumptions that underlie our retributive system. It seeks to deinstitutionalize abstract and ineffective systems of jurisprudence and replace them with practical action by concrete, grassroots communities.

Restorative justice is not a program, or a specific way of doing things, although there are, of course, programs consistent with its principles. It is, rather, a perspective, a point of view, a focus from which we can better understand the realities of crime and punishment in our society. Restorative justice represents what philosophers call a "paradigm shift," or a change in explanatory models, in how to think about crime, violence, and conflict—and how to respond.

Restorative justice is also a movement—one that goes well beyond the criminal justice system and beyond the United States. The theoretical framework and practical expressions of restorative justice have been shaped primarily in the arena of the criminal justice systems of the United States and other English-speaking nations. Although they were designed specifically as alter-

natives to those prevailing systems, some of the most notable examples of restorative justice are carried out in very different contexts. The basic principles of restorative justice apply to many other interpersonal disputes and to many larger conflicts between ethnic groups, nations, labor and management, and political factions. The work of the Truth and Reconciliation Commission in post-apartheid South Africa is a prime example of restorative justice. But for our purposes the distinctiveness of the approach can best be understood by contrasting it with the criminal justice system in the United States.

We will begin to spell out this contrast very shortly. But first we need to take a close look at Jesus—who he is and what he is about—for it is from him that we who seek to follow (not merely worship) him must take our guidance.

Soon after Jesus rode into Jerusalem to face execution at the hands of the legal, political, and religious establishments of his day, he entered the temple. There, angered by the idolatry of wealth (Luke 16:13c), he overturned the tables of the money changers and denounced those who had turned God's sacred place into "a den of robbers" (Matthew 21:12-13). It was a prophetic act of indignant, righteous anger. Some biblical scholars believe it was the final straw that caused his enemies to decide he must be done away with as an enemy of the state and the dominant religious institutions of the culture. Soon thereafter, Jesus again turned the tables on the powerful of his time and place when he drew a distinction between that which is Caesar's, i.e., the state's, and that which is God's (Matthew 22:15-22).

Earlier, as we read in John's gospel, Jesus had

confounded those who wanted him to approve the legal execution of a woman caught in adultery. Jesus reframes the question from "Does she deserve to be killed?" to "Which of you deserves to kill her?" (John 8:2-11, RSV).

As he was being put to death, Jesus not only asked God to forgive his executioners (Luke 23:24), but promised the repentant bandit on the cross next to his, that, regardless of Caesar's and Pilate's actions, they would be together in Paradise (Luke 23:39-43).

At various points in Jesus' teaching ministry, he told his followers that they were to love their enemies (Matthew 5:43-48); refrain from judging other persons (Matthew 7:1-5); forgive infinitely (Matthew 18:21-22); minister to victims of crime (Luke 10:25-37); visit the prisoners (Matthew 25:32-46); heal the sick—even if it involves breaking laws (Luke 6:6-11; 9:1-6); turn the other cheek when assaulted (Matthew 5:38-42); and follow Jesus in the Jubilee tradition of proclaiming and enacting liberty to the captives (Luke 4:16-21).

In all of these examples, Jesus challenged what Paul later called the "principalities and powers" (Romans 8:38-39; Ephesians 6:12) dominant in his religious, political, and legal culture: "For our struggle is not against enemies of blood and flesh, but against the rulers, against the authorities, against the cosmic powers of this present darkness, against the spiritual forces of evil in the heavenly places" (Ephesians 6:12).

Jesus took on the system—as he did throughout his life—most sharply in his death. He practiced the politics of prophesy, embodying the link between spirituality and direct action. And, if we are attentive, he redefined for us the terms of what we mean by criminal justice.

What does Jesus have to do with the massive network of laws, courts, jails, prisons, and bureaucracies that make up what we call our criminal justice system? To address this question, it is necessary to look at the developing philosophy of restorative justice, for it is the direct opposite of our dominant criminal justice system and its obsession with retribution.

This retributive system has been described by Mark Umbreit, of the Minneapolis-based Center for Restorative Justice and Mediation, as rooted in a "kind of trail 'em, nail 'em, jail 'em mentality." Howard Zehr summarizes this system in terms of the questions it asks after a crime has been committed: "What laws have been broken? Who done it? What punishment does he deserve?" Zehr suggests a very different set of questions from the perspective of restorative justice: "Who has been hurt? What are their needs? Whose obligation is it to meet their needs?" ("Restoring Justice," video, Presbyterian Church U.S.A., 1996)

Our current system, based on the concept of retribution or revenge, defines crime primarily as an offense against the laws of the state, which considers itself the victim of any crime. This is reflected in the convention of calling criminal cases "*State of _____ vs. _____*." The state, in turn, assumes the power of picking out a likely offender and processing that person through an adversarial drama in which the major actors are lawyers. Through either a plea-bargaining process behind the scenes, or a trial in open court played out according to rules established by the state and enforced by the judge, the opposing attorneys fight it out in a sort of war game. Eventually the accused is declared guilty or not guilty. If the person is found to be, or pleads, guilty, a sentence is imposed. That sentence may amount to a symbolic slap on the wrist (simple probation), a highly punitive prison term, ritual killing by the state, or something in-between.

The focus is on the offender and on the offender's past behavior. The real victim of the crime—if there is a victim—is treated as marginal, as is the community, except to the extent that they can be manipulated into lobbying for vengeance. The offender is treated as a passive participant. The process is geared toward fixing blame, not solving problems. The relationship between the victim and the offender—whether there was one before the crime, or whether it was established by the crime—is ignored. Repentance and forgiveness are discouraged. Accountability in this context means that the offender takes the assigned punishment passively.

The whole process encourages competitive and individualistic values; assumes a "win-lose" outcome; and ignores the social, economic, political, cultural, and moral context of the crime and what would constitute an appropriate response to it. It is based on a commitment to retribution by the state against the offender, not on the principle of restitution by the offender to the victim. Opportunities abound for abuse of discretion and for corruption, racism, sexism, and class discrimination—personal and institutional. In the current system, it is increasingly the prosecuting attorney who has the lion's share of discretionary power.

In the face of this system of retributive justice, the alternative perspective of restorative justice raises critical questions:

- Who is the real victim of a crime? Is it the state, as in our present criminal justice system? Or is it the person whose body, soul, and/or property were violated?

- What is real accountability? Is it passively "taking your punishment"? Or is it taking responsibility for making the situation "right," insofar as possible; for making restitution to the person one has violated?

- Can or should a people that has been systematically violated and oppressed "forgive and forget"? Or does true healing and reconciliation require remembering, truth-telling, and forgiveness?

- In what ways do we want criminals to change? To make sure not to get caught next time (the likeliest result of a punitive approach)? Or to develop a degree of internal self-discipline that will help them control their behavior?

- How can we best bring about change in people? By intentionally inflicting pain upon them? (The words "punish" and "pain" have the same Greek root meaning "payment" or " penalty.") Can we get people to change by literally "scaring the hell out of them"—the theory behind the notion of deterrence? Or do people change most deeply by being loved and having some reason to hope for a better life?

- What socioeconomic conditions help to generate crime and violence in our communities? What underlying corporate and political systems are responsible for those conditions? How can we transform poor—and wealthy—communities, erasing massive economic inequality?

- Who has the most at stake in determining what

is required "to make it right," insofar as possible, after a crime has been committed? Who ought to be principally involved in making such decisions? A group of lawyers—or the victims, the victimizers, and persons in the local community?

■ When violations of human rights have been committed by those in power, how can this truth be told and publicly acknowledged?

Restorative justice reverses the system of retributive justice at almost every point. Crime is understood primarily as the violation of one person by another—or, by extension, as the violation of a person or a group by an institution or a system. The real victim, the offender, and the local community are seen as the principal stakeholders. Therefore, they are the ones principally involved in deciding what it will take to "make it right." Their relationships and their feelings are seriously regarded. A future, problem-solving, healing orientation predominates. Accountability is understood to be the taking of responsibility for what one has done, repenting of it, trying to "make it right" (typically through restitution by the offender to the victim), and not doing it again. Dialogue—not an adversarial battle—is the norm.

In restorative justice, the community takes responsibility for helping the offender and the victim "work it out" in ways they both can live with, and holds the offender responsible for following through with whatever that entails. And, even as the community supports the victim, it seeks to help the offender meet his/her needs. Instead of rejection, the community seeks the offender's integration into its fabric.

Restorative justice examines the total context of the situation, rather than the crime as an isolat-

ed event. Just as it seeks to empower victims, it seeks to empower offenders by fostering in them remorse because of their violation of others. Restorative justice encourages internal self-discipline instead of passive acceptance of externally imposed punishment. This is in stark contrast to mere regret by offenders that they were caught, perceiving themselves victims of the criminal justice system. Restorative justice teaches victim, offender, and community new ways of dealing with conflict.

Restorative justice encourages cooperation, striving for "win-win" outcomes rather than buying into the "win-lose" model of the adversarial, retributive system (in practice, more often a "lose-lose" proposition). Instead of the unrealistic "forgive and forget" model, or the vengeful one of "remember and punish," restorative justice offers a healing vision of "remember, restore, and reconcile" for all the principal parties: victim, offender, and community.

Rather than escalating the cycle of violence and coercion by both individuals and institutions, restorative justice tries to stop it in its tracks. Rather than separating legal or criminal justice from the larger picture of distributive justice— that is, how wealth, power, and status are portioned out among different groups in society— restorative justice looks at the whole social, historical, and political context to determine how the law can be most fairly applied, and how it needs to be rewritten.

Thus, a community shaped by the perspective of restorative justice takes responsibility not only for responding to a particular crime in a healing way. It also seeks to change the economic, cultural, and political structures responsible for policies and practices resulting in inequitable distribution of wealth, status, and power. Together with the offender's personal responsibility, it is these inequities that are among the root causes of crime in the streets—as well as crime in the suites. In individual cases as well as in a broader, systemic sense, restorative justice promotes reintegration instead of marginalization or polarization for both victims and offenders. At its best, restorative justice is alert to certain harmful community patterns that may emerge while examining particular cases within its framework. This is especially true of "circle sentencing," a process to be considered later in this chapter.

Let us summarize. *Retributive justice* defines crime as breaking the law of the state and owing a debt to society. *Restorative justice* defines crime as the violation of another by a person or organization. According to the method of restorative justice, that person or organization then owes a debt to the victim as well as to the local community. Retributive justice empowers professionals (primarily lawyers) to make decisions about victims, offenders, and local communities. Restorative justice helps victims, offenders, and local communities—the primary stakeholders—to decide the right course of action when a person or organization has violated another.

A justice system based on restoration would look very different from the one we have. Such a system would not be "warm and fuzzy," characterized by an "I'm okay, you're okay" attitude. Nor would it be "soft on crime." It would perhaps be more akin to the tough-love approach or the 12-step addiction recovery model, in which a critical step for healing is making amends to those one has violated. Emotionally, physically, and spiritually, a restorative justice solution often requires very hard work by the offender. The same is true, of course, for the victim. But a system rooted in such an approach would be more just in responding to crime, more preventive in its long-term outcomes, and more effective in educating and empowering all parties to analyze and transform the forces acting upon them.

If a restorative rather than retributive justice system were in place, there would be many more opportunities for offenders and victims to struggle face-to-face, in the presence of community mediators, over what one has done to the other, and why; and what they now need to do about it, with the support of the community. There would be vastly fewer opportunities for under-the-table deal-making, courtroom theatrics, gamesmanship by lawyers and judges, and "quick-fix" law-and-order rhetoric by politicians looking for easy votes.

We would have fewer courtrooms and jails, and more neighborhood-based dispute mediation centers. There would be fewer cops and more local volunteer mediators. Fewer guns and bullets, more talk. Adequate education and treatment programs for alcohol and drug addiction instead of war on some of the people who use drugs (overwhelmingly young, poor, urban, African American). No private for-profit prisons, but fewer and better publicly operated prisons. No more prison-building boom, but more community-based alternative programs. No death penalty, but more restitution to victims. Less crime, more dialogue. More victims' rights, but not the right to revenge. And no victims' rights at the expense of defendants' rights. No more sentence-enhancement hate-crime legislation, but less hate.

So, what does restorative justice look like in practice? On the Western scene, specifically in the realm of criminal justice, the 320 or so victim-offender mediation programs (VOMPs) in communities throughout Canada and the United States, and the 700 in Europe, are good examples. Such VOMPs use trained volunteers as mediators in selected, court-referred cases. These consist of face-to-face dialogue between willing crime victims and their victimizers, who must take some responsibility for the offense. They ask questions of one another, express their feelings, and struggle—with the mediators' help—to come to a fair resolution they can both accept. It may involve direct financial restitution, community service, drug/alcohol treatment, or other options. The signed agreement is then reported to the court, and may become all or part of the sentence or a condition for pre-trial diversion or probation. Compliance with the agreement is monitored by the VOMP staff or the court.

Many of these victim-offender mediation programs call themselves victim-offender reconciliation programs (VORPs), reflecting the origin of many in faith communities. In recent years, however, there has been a move toward using the more neutral name, "victim-offender mediation program", which describes the process, rather than the hoped-for outcome.

Victims choosing to participate in mediation have the opportunity to ask the offenders questions and tell how they feel about what was done to them. Offenders choosing to participate have the opportunity to learn more about how their actions have affected the victims and, if so moved, to express their remorse directly to those whom they have hurt. Usually the two parties, with the help of the mediators, work out an agreement about what would "make it right," sign a contract to that effect, and move on with their lives.

In most of these cases, victims and offenders experience a kind of real justice that is hard to find in a courtroom where lawyers and judges, rather than those most directly involved, have the power to make decisions. But sometimes more than justice takes place in these encounters. Sometimes there is true reconciliation. Sometimes there are hugs and tears of grief and joy.

Besides victim-offender mediation, usually involving one or two mediators, the victim and the offender (and in the case of a juvenile offender or victim, their parents), there are other techniques and methods informed by a restorative justice perspective. These include family group conferencing, circle sentencing, and community reparative boards.

Family group conferencing is based on the traditional processes of dispute resolution practiced by the Maori, aborigines of New Zealand. In 1989 it became an official part of New Zealand's justice system, and one version is extensively used in southern Australia. In the United States, family group conferencing is used in a number of communities in Minnesota and Pennsylvania, as well as some other states. It usually involves the victim, the offender (usually a juvenile), key family members of each, and other key persons in the lives of each. Often it includes police, teachers, and others who represent the community. The group is convened by a trained facilitator. Participants describe how they have been affected by the crime, as well as ways in which the offender can repair the injury to both victim and community, with the support of those in the room. The process can be an alternative to, or used in conjunction with, traditional court proceedings. Participation is voluntary.

Similarly, circle sentencing is based on the traditional processes of Canadian aboriginal groups and American Indians. It is most frequently used in several provinces of Canada and in Minnesota. In the words of Mark Umbreit and Gordon Bazemore, it is "a holistic reintegrative strategy designed not only to address the criminal and delinquent behavior of offenders but also to consider the needs of victims, families, and communities."

Circles, facilitated by a trained "keeper," typically involve a cast of characters similar to family group conferences. Often there are several gatherings, and the process can be extremely labor-intensive. Primary goals include healing for all parties, making amends by the offender, building a sense of community, and addressing the causes of the criminal behavior. Circle sentencing is employed in more serious cases, and more often with repeat offenders, than is the norm for the other methods discussed here.

Since 1966, community reparative boards have been used extensively as a central part of the criminal and juvenile justice systems in Vermont. These are generally more formal boards made up of small groups of local citizens who are given extensive training. Cases are referred by the courts, and the boards hold public meetings involving the offenders (who are court-ordered to participate), with some participation by victims. The boards then deliberate privately and develop proposals for sanctions which are negotiated with the offender until an agreement is reached. The boards monitor the offender's compliance with the contracts and report back to the court.

Of all the models employing an approach of restorative justice, the voluntary offender mediation programs (VOMPs) have received the greatest degree of formal evaluation. A large four-site study of juvenile VOMPs done in the early 1990s found extremely positive results:

- 95 percent of mediation sessions produced a negotiated restitution contract.

- 79 percent of victims were satisfied with the process, compared to 57 percent of victims in non-mediated cases.

- Post-mediation, victims were considerably less fearful of subsequent victimization.

- 81 percent of offenders completed their restitution obligations established in mediation, compared with 58 percent of offenders when the restitution was imposed by the court.

- Offenders who had gone through mediation had an 18-percent recidivism rate, compared to 27 percent of those whose cases were not mediated.

- The seriousness of crimes committed after the present one was higher for those offenders who had not participated in mediation.

Studies done of other restorative justice models report findings consistent with the above.

To be sure, not every criminal case lends itself

to resolution by mediation or other forms of restorative justice, no matter how effective they may be in selected cases. Even as research and evaluations continue, an official legal system needs to remain in place as a backup when mediation or other strategies of restorative justice fail. Furthermore, an official system is needed to handle cases for which restorative justice techniques are not appropriate. In cases involving domestic violence and sexual abuse, for example, the complex emotional dynamics and the major differences in power of victim and victimizer do not easily lend themselves to such an approach.

The official system of justice must also play the critical role of monitoring the deliberately less formal efforts of restorative justice, in order to ensure the protection of everyone's constitutional rights. And safeguards are needed to make sure that on the grassroots community level, restorative justice does not become revenge-driven vigilante justice. However, as its undergirding principle, restorative justice insists that the focus of any good justice system be on the primary stakeholders themselves, not on the professionals acting in their behalf.

As we have seen, retributive justice keeps victims and offenders apart, pitting them against each other. Restorative justice seeks to create a situation in which persons or groups in conflict can meet face-to-face, engaging in dialogue and negotiation. This normally includes victim, offender, and representatives of the local community. They are encouraged to deal with one another directly, not just through professionals acting as their representatives (lawyers or official diplomats). This promotes problem-solving rather than

an adversarial, military-style approach. It looks toward the future, not just the past. It is not content with fixing blame and punishing someone, but fosters repentance, reconciliation, and healing for all parties and relationships in a given situation.

One of the basic differences between retributive and restorative justice is this: retributive justice regards victims and offenders as two separate groups; that it is possible to care for one or the other, but not for both. Restorative justice sees both victims and offenders as human beings oppressed by the system of retributive justice. It is the task of restorative justice to search for common ground between victim and offender, recognizing that many offenders have themselves been victims, and that many victims have been offenders.

Within the context of the criminal justice system, activities informed and guided by a commitment to restorative justice may include ministering with the incarcerated, but its scope goes far beyond prison ministry. It includes involvement in the many other points in the system where decisions affecting offenders, victims, and the community as a whole are made. It also encompasses ministry with crime victims, with the families of victims and offenders, and with those who work within the criminal and juvenile justice systems. For all of these persons and groups it offers support and accountability, comforting the afflicted and afflicting the comfortable. Whatever the context, restorative justice strives for the fine balance of being, in the words of Jesus, "wise as a serpent and gentle as a dove."

Earlier we noted that certain methods of restorative justice have their roots in aboriginal traditions of communal dispute resolution, as well as in the Hebrew and Christian Scriptures. It is the tradition of Jubilee, as spelled out most thoroughly in Leviticus 25, in which the concept of restorative justice has much of its Judeo-Christian scriptural basis. Biblical scholar and theologian Walter Brueggemann argues as follows: "In biblical faith, the doing of justice is the primary expectation of God," and his rendering of biblical justice, based on the Jubilee model, is this: "Justice is to sort out what belongs to whom, and to return it to them. . . . So the work of liberation, redemption, salvation, is the work of giving things back" (Walter Brueggemann, Sharon Parks, and Thomas H. Groome, *To Act Justly, Love Tenderly, Walk Humbly: An Agenda for Ministers*. New York: Paulist Press, 1986).

Theologian Karen Lebacqz, in her book *Justice in an Unjust World*, emphasizes the two sides of restorative justice as captured in the Jubilee tradition: "The Jubilee year . . . [s]eems to be an image appropriate for justice in an unjust world. It is an image that captures the two sides of justice emerging from injustice: the liberation that characterizes justice from the perspective of the oppressed, and the restitution that characterizes justice from the perspective of the oppressor. At root, the Jubilee expresses the covenant notion that all are mutually accountable."

In her book *Proclaim Jubilee: Spirituality for the 21st Century* (Louisville: Westminster, John Knox, 1996), Maria Harris writes that originally one of the Hebrew words for justice, *mispat*, probably "referred to the restoration of a situation or an environment that promoted equity and harmony—*shalom*—in a community. . . . It refers to basic human rights and to the restorative acts of repair-

ing the world." In language that makes explicit what this restorative nature of biblical Jubilee justice entails—whether for the individual criminal or for the affluent classes and nations—Harris echoes Brueggemann and spells out what his insight means when applied not just to a thief, but to a whole people—perhaps even the people of North America:

> The particular meaning of justice that Jubilee stresses is the notion of "return," not in the Jubilee journey sense of return home but return as relinquishing, giving back, and handing over what is not ours to God and to those crying for justice throughout the whole, round earth.

In this way it can be seen how at its earliest biblical origin, restorative justice does not limit itself to the particular crime or offense at hand, but, rather, broadens and deepens the focus to take account of the whole historical context of systemic inequity in the distribution of goods—economic, political, and cultural—among groups.

At one point Harris specifically takes up the Jubilee call for the liberation of captives, as presented in Leviticus 25:10 and 24, and in later references to the Jubilee tradition in Isaiah 61:1 and, of course, Luke 4:18. She acknowledges the following:

> In the Bible, prisoners are not criminals or convicts, because incarceration was not the penalty for civilian criminal acts. Rather, they were prisoners of war or of conscience, debtors, captives, hostages, victims of militarism or government oppression. . . .

Not all prisoners today are innocent good guys—they have done terrible things. Still, the command stands: Proclaim liberty throughout the land to all its inhabitants; free the prisoners from bondage. We who are Jews and Christians and have a long line of convicted felons in our religious ancestry need to find ways . . . to help these prisoners return home.

To this, I would add three points:

1. Whenever possible, we need to help offenders find ways to return what they have taken from their victims.

2. Not all prisoners today are guilty, nor—even if guilty—are they evil people.

3. When a nation like ours locks up two million human beings, disproportionately the poor and people of color, it is no longer such a stretch to see many of them in their own way as "prisoners of war . . ., debtors, captives, hostages, victims of militarism or government oppression," in Harris' words.

If the Jubilee tradition provides part of the biblical basis for restorative justice, another central concept, closely associated with Jubilee, is that of *shalom*. This ancient Hebrew word, often translated as "peace," actually means something more like "whole and right relationships," or "peace with justice," including elements of fairness and equity between persons and between groups as well as the good feeling of harmony. One close translation, in the words of a popular bumper sticker, might be, "If you want peace, work for justice." In keeping with this twofold emphasis, the Communities of Shalom initiative of The United Methodist Church began in 1992 at the church's General Conference. The quadrennial gathering took place that year immediately following the violent rebellion in South Central Los Angeles set off by the jury verdict in the first Rodney King police brutality case. The concept *shalom* captures both the need for justice/righteousness/fairness—one component of the restorative justice vision, and the hope for love/mercy/reconciliation—the other component of that vision.

In a groundbreaking essay, the late Virginia Mackey, an early North American pioneer in restorative justice, wrote of the Jewish tradition:

The Judaic connotation of justice (*tsedeqah*)is one of that which "makes things right." Divine justice (*tsedeq*) is synonymous with holiness or righteousness. Human justice (*tsedeqah*) is "rightness." In their Scripture and tradition, Jews have urged caution in judgment, have shown reluctance to punish, and have exhibited the desire to make atonement, restitution, or reconciliation when conflicts have occurred. This is their interpretation of "making right," "making peace," or achieving *shalom*. The predominant theology is one of restoration

In a paper presented at the National Religious Leaders Consultation on Criminal Justice, Claremont, California, September 1981, Rolf Knierim spells out in terms of the Hebrew Bible the offender's part of the responsibility for restoring *shalom*:

The Old Testament clearly speaks about restitution. If a thief steals his neighbor's ox (and provided he is caught), he has to return the ox, or to replace it and to pay a fine. He has to make "restitution." The Hebrew term used in this connection, *shillem*, which is related to *shalom*, means literally to make the (original) situation full, to restore it. Thus, reconciliation involves an act of restoration which requires restitution by the evildoer and sometimes even a fine. It involves the evildoer's share in the process of reconciliation, and not only the forgiving acceptance of him by the damaged party or community, so that the original situation of wholeness = peace can be restored. In the New Testament there are certain key passages concerning issues of crime and punishment. We have mentioned the Parable of the Good Samaritan (Luke 10:25-37), which gives a clear mandate for practical, compassionate Christian ministry with crime victims. Similarly, the Parable of the Last Judgment (Matthew 25:31-48) lifts up the ministry of presence with those in prison as a distinctive mark of faithful discipleship. Finally, the Parable of the Workers in the Vineyard (Matthew 20:1-16), makes clear that in the eyes of God there is more to the concept of justice than how it is usually defined.

New Testament passages concerning issues of crime and punishment include three parables: the Good Samaritan (Luke 10: 25-37), the Last Judgment (Matthew 25:31-48), and the Workers in the Vineyard (Matthew 20: 1-16). Paul's epistles also yield passages that express a restorative, reconciling spirit, as the following examples demonstrate: Romans 12:17-21 deals critically with the human desire for vengeance. In 2 Corinthians 5:16-21 we find Paul's great discourse on how the cosmic reconciliation wrought by God in Jesus Christ changes everything and makes all human beings brothers and sisters reconciled to one another, whether we like it or not. Galatians 6:1 spells out how we should "restore" one who transgresses "in a spirit of gentleness," taking care that we ourselves "are not tempted."

Other passages throughout the New Testament speak to these concerns. In Hebrews 13:3, solidarity with strangers, prisoners, and victims of torture is lifted up as a virtue. In Luke 19:1-10, the story of Zacchaeus, the cheating tax collector, demonstrates how the response toward restitution and restoration grows out of a genuine inner conviction of sin, and of forgiveness through personal encounter with Jesus. Finally, there is Matthew 18: 15-22, in which a version of mediation or circle sentencing is offered in dealing with conflict in the Christian faith community.

Our United Methodist heritage echoes the biblical concern for restoring justice. When John Wesley was alive in 18th-century England, the criminal justice system was retributive in the extreme. According to the late Bishop Gerald Kennedy (Introduction to John Wesley's *Journals*), there were 253 offenses which could carry the death penalty, including shooting a rabbit, damaging a bridge, cutting down a young tree, or stealing anything that was worth five shillings or more. Debtors were frequently held in prison, where the conditions were abominable. John's father, Samuel, who had visited prisoners in the prisons of Oxford in the 1680s as a student at Exeter, actually himself served time in debtors' prison in 1705. While at Oxford, the brothers John and Charles Wesley began a lifelong ministry of visiting prisoners once or twice a week. They were sometimes able to get prisoners released by paying the remaining debts of those who were there for owing small sums.

In 1735, the Wesley brothers journeyed as missionaries with Colonel James Edward Oglethorpe to Oglethorpe's colony for formerly imprisoned English debtors in what is now the state of Georgia. After the time in Georgia, which did not go well for him, John grew increasingly troubled about his soul and his faith.

On March 6, 1738, John Wesley offered salvation by faith alone to a death-sentenced prisoner named Clifford. In his journal entry for March 27, Wesley reported that Clifford had died "in perfect peace." On May 24, Wesley had a decisive spiritual experience at a meeting on Aldersgate Street, where he reached the perfect peace of trust and the assurance of forgiveness.

Wesley's journals continue to reflect the frequency and importance of prison ministry based on the Parable of the Last Judgment. During one nine-month period, he preached at least sixty-seven times in various prisons and jails. Prison visitation was seen by John Wesley and others as so important a feature of the life of Christian discipleship that a 1778 Conference made prison visitation obligatory for all Methodist preachers.

Bishop Kenneth Carder has reminded more recent United Methodists that the Wesleys spent much more time at [London's] Newgate Prison than at Aldersgate Street, adding that a case can be made that Newgate Prison and the other prisons across England were as decisive in sparking the Methodist revival as was the experience at Aldersgate.

Home Cooking Leads to Love of Inmates

They look tough at first, with their muscle shirts, tattoos, and striped prison pants. Ask, and the inmates might tell you why they're serving time: selling pot, facilitating murder, or aggravated rape and kidnapping.

It's a beautiful day in Mountain City, Tennessee, as a prison guard watches the men put up dry-wall and install window casings at Valley View United Methodist Church. Nearby, churchwomen are laying out a home-cooked meal in the fellowship hall. The men might have to be tough at Northeastern Correctional Complex, the 1700-inmate facility where they'll return at the end of the day, but here they are humble—one might even say sweet. "These prisoners are so tender," said the Rev. Bill Cahill, Mountain City Circuit pastor. "Our ladies get a blessing out of their coming here."

For more than a year, Cahill has managed to get his Abingdon District churches—Valley View, Doe Valley, and Shouns—on the schedule of a community service crew from Northeastern that does short-term construction projects. It's a terrific arrangement. The churches buy their own supplies and provide the inmates' meals. They save thousands of dollars on skilled labor and get a chance to minister to people who obviously appreciate it.

"They treat us so good," said Rick Latham, 46, a native of Townsend, Tennessee. "They want to feed us everything you can imagine, all home-cooked. I love it, but it makes me homesick."

Inmates have to work their way up a point system and demonstrate a level of skill before they can be placed on one of five construction crews at Northeastern, according to Sgt. Bill Williams, who schedules and oversees the projects. Crew members say they like being on the outside, working with their hands, breathing fresh air. They look forward to Monday morning. They use words like "tense" and "stressful" to describe where they spend their nights. "This is as close to freedom as you can get when you're doing time," said Mark Brown, 32, of Green Bay, Wisconsin. When he gets out of Northeastern—maybe in two months, probably in three years—the experience he's gained as a dry-wall worker will come in handy. Until his release, Brown likes helping Valley View members and other nonprofit groups in the area. Like the other men, he's proud of the buildings he's worked on. "It gives my life meaning," he said. "I'm doing something purposeful for somebody now."

Parishioners aren't supposed to witness to the inmates, Cahill said, but the women who cook for them feel so close to them over time, "they can't help but share the love of Jesus."

"They are so gracious and respectful and always thankful," said Valley View member Pauline Phillippi of the men who have replaced the roof and built a garage for the parsonage. "We thoroughly enjoy having them here."

The Mountain City Circuit churches have also created ministries for inmates' families who have recently relocated to the area, collecting clothes, opening a food pantry and donating school supplies. The Holston Annual Conference of the United Methodist Church recently offered to send inmates' children to Camp Ahistadi for a free week of summer camp.

Some communities complain about having a prison nearby, "but this community has been blessed by it," said Abingdon District Superintendent Brenda Carroll. "They've been changed as they've discovered new ministries to serve these men and their families. It's a beautiful thing to see."

(A UMNS feature in 2001 by Annette Spencer Bender, editor of *The Call*, newspaper of The United Methodist Church's Holston Annual Conference.)

"The work of mediation and conflict transformation is spiritual work, and must be grounded in a ministry of reconciliation."

—Rev. Tom Porter

3

FINDING RESTORATIVE JUSTICE IN CHURCHES, CONFERENCES, AND COMMUNITIES

We have painted a bleak picture of the retributive state of criminal justice in the United States. We have also lifted up the vision of restorative justice as a promising alternative to the failed system. But there are questions:

■ What does restorative justice look like in practice?

■ Where is restorative justice actually being done?

■ Where are United Methodists engaging in restorative justice?

■ Who are they?

■ What are they doing?

In this chapter we present profiles that demonstrate the wide and rich variety of what is possible when communities, agencies, individuals, and churches catch a glimpse of or stumble into a better way of responding to conflict, crime, and violence. According to Minnesota restorative justice advocate and practitioner Kay Pranis, "Restorative justice is not a program or a cluster of programs. It is a way of working with victims, offenders, and communities to achieve the goal of repairing the harm to the degree possible."

In this chapter we learn how some people are trying to repair the harm done by crime, as well as by punishment. A few of these ministries actually emphasize engagement and dialogue between victims and offenders, which is a mark of restorative justice in its classic form. Others do not, but are clearly done from the perspective and the values of restorative justice.

1. *Tennessee: A Local Prison Ministry Grows and Flourishes.* Henry Harrison is a businessman—president of Concrete Products Co., Inc., Jackson, Tennessee. But he is also a member of Jackson's First United Methodist Church, and—even more important—a serious Christian. For more than ten years he has coordinated a class in what he calls life skills masonry for male and female prisoners at the Madison County Penal Farm. The heart of the ministry is summarized by Mr. Harrison: "It's wonderful to see what God can do when we trust his guidance. Over a ten-week period, we transform lives and simultaneously build a workforce for Madison County."

Partially funded by the Job Training Partnership Act, the ministry succeeds mostly because of the volunteer work of First Church members and staff, local UMC ministers, retired workers from Mr. Harrison's business, and staff of local social agencies. In addition to teaching prisoners a marketable trade—sometimes masonry, sometimes other trades in construction—the program helps them find work upon their release.

Harrison and other church and community volunteers also offer a personal growth and development school: ecumenically staffed classes in spiritual growth, human reproduction, causes/prevention/control of sexually transmitted diseases, budgeting, anger control, civics, personal hygiene, parliamentary procedure, drug abuse, and ergonomics.

In ten years, the program has graduated 175 men and women, of whom all but five have found good jobs. The known rate of recidivism is minuscule. The program is so successful that in the year 2000, Madison County sheriff David Woolfork asked Harrison to speak about the program at the Tennessee Sheriffs' Association, and encouraged his peers to help develop similar programs in the state's other ninety-four counties.

Graduation ceremonies for the year 2000, at First Church, were attended by the local sheriff, the district attorney, the public defender, First Church's pastor, and the United Methodist district superintendent, as well as staff from the Memphis conference and the General Board of Global Ministries' office of restorative justice ministries. Volunteer teacher Billy Joe Winslow told the graduates, "All the goodies are upstream, and you have to swim against the current to get to them. The more you do that, the better off you'll be." Not a bad definition of Christian discipleship.

The ten graduating inmates presented Henry Harrison with an autographed brick paperweight bearing these words: "We have limited resources, but unlimited creativity." Their spokesman told Harrison and the other volunteers, "You recognized our wrongdoing but didn't constantly throw it back in our face, but tried to help us." Not a bad description of God's gracious, restorative justice.

2. *Oklahoma: Criminal Justice and Mercy Ministries* (CJAMM). In Oklahoma there are many people in prison. In the year 2000, it ranked third among all states in its rate of incarceration. But at least the church—specifically, The United Methodist Church—is there, as well. Of all annual

conferences in the denomination, the Oklahoma Annual Conference has what is probably the most extensive program of ministries in the criminal justice arena.

The Oklahoma conference's Criminal Justice and Mercy Ministries (CJAMM) is directed by Rev. Stan Basler, a former criminal defense lawyer. CJAMM receives funding from the conference, the General Board of Global Ministries, and other sources. In the year 2000, CJAMM employed four full-time and eight part-time staff people as well as numerous volunteers.

CJAMM's ministries include the following:

■ A United Methodist ministry presence in every prison in the state: Yokefellow groups, Covenant Discipleship groups, Kairos weekends.

■ Redemption churches—composed of minimum security prisoners, ex-offenders, prisoners' family members, and local United Methodists and other Christians—in Tulsa, Oklahoma City, and Lawton. Programs include 12-step recovery groups, cognitive therapy, literacy training, and parenting classes. Claudia Lovelace, chairperson of Oklahoma City's Penn Redemption Church's pastor/staff-parish relations committee, credits her participation in this congregation with turning her life around. A survivor of sexual abuse, a former prostitute, and a recovering drug/alcohol addict, she is now a counselor at a drug rehabilitation center where, she says, she can identify with almost anyone there. "I take everything that has happened in my life—including the bad stuff—as a gift that God can use to help someone through me," she says.

■ Annual New Day camps for prisoners' children ages 8 to 11 and 12 to 14, that attract numerous volunteers.

■ Exodus House, a programmed residential facility for ex-prisoners, offering six months of rent-free housing, 12-step programs, and other services. Exodus House is attached to and coordinated with the local Redemption Church in order to insure the community's continuity after residents leave the house.

■ Juvenile Offender Ministries, which encompass a variety of ministries with poor, troubled, drop-out, and ex-offender youth.

■ Justice advocacy ministries, mostly in coalition with other church and criminal justice groups, including an annual "Day at the Legislature."

3. *Nationwide: Murder Victims' Families for Reconciliation (MFVR)*. When Rev. Walter Everett, a United Methodist pastor in Hartford, Connecticut, speaks or preaches, he emphasizes that the death penalty is "both morally wrong and counterproductive." Most people listen, because a man named Mike shot and killed Everett's son Scott on July 26, 1987. Everett went through all the usual stages of anger and grief. Finally, turning it over to God, he was able through "not a feeling, but an act of the will," to forgive Mike—eventually testifying on Mike's behalf for his release, and officiating at his wedding.

Now Everett is a member of the board of directors of Murder Victims' Families for Reconciliation (MVFR), which was founded in 1976 by Marie Deans and has become a unique component of the national struggle for abolition of the death penalty. To its great credit, MVFR's membership includes survivors of state killing, i.e., execution, as well as murder carried out by individuals. This gives the group high credibility when it speaks with one voice in its absolute opposition to the death penalty for anyone, anywhere.

MVFR members' common ground ensures that while the organization's primary goal is an end to capital punishment, it also offers support for victims of murder and works with other victims' groups and death penalty abolition groups. MVFR and its members testify in legislatures and courtrooms, but they also educate criminal justice groups, faith communities, civic organizations, educators, and journalists through their speakers' bureau and staff. The organization held its first national conference in 2001, publishes a newsletter, *The Voice*, and continues to print new editions of *Not in Our Name: Murder Victims' Families Speak Out Against the Death Penalty*, an extraordinary book of profiles, photos, and quotes by its members.

MVFR has achieved perhaps its greatest visibility through the public witness of its frequent spokesperson, Bud Welch, an Oklahoma City gas station owner and Catholic layman. Welch discovered the beginning of healing and, as he says, came closest to God when he befriended Timothy McVeigh's father and sister after his own daughter Julie was killed in the 1995 Oklahoma City bombing. Welch kept his promise to Bill McVeigh by doing everything he could to prevent Timothy McVeigh's execution, because he knew, as he frequently said before it happened, "As far as the death penalty is concerned, it won't help me any when Tim McVeigh is killed. The death penalty is

about revenge and hate, and revenge and hate is why my daughter and those 167 other people are dead today."

MVFR is eager to help interested groups organize state and local chapters throughout the country, and has expanded its staff to build its organizing capacity. In many towns and cities individuals who have lost loved ones to murder or execution reject capital punishment, but often face opposition, hostility, and misunderstanding. Most of them know nothing about MVFR, or even that many others in their position feel as they do. It could be an important ministry for United Methodists—who have churches almost everywhere in the United States—to seek out such folk, link them with one another, and connect them to MVFR. It would be a way of helping them find support and healing, and move us all another step toward achieving one of our own Social Principles: "We oppose capital punishment and urge its elimination from all criminal codes" (*The Book of Discipline of The United Methodist Church*, Nashville: The United Methodist Publishing House, 2000, p. 117).

4. *Pennsylvania: People United Together* (PUT). Along with the Fortune Society in New York City, and the Delancey Street Foundation on the West Coast, People United Together, (PUT) has blazed new trails in the area of prisoner reintegration into the community. PUT was founded in 1990 by a group of ex-prisoners who had collaborated in advocating for better prison conditions while incarcerated during the 1980s at Pennsylvania's Holmesburg Prison. With help from the Pennsylvania Prison Society and Rev. Robin

Hynicka, then pastor of Cookman United Methodist Church in Philadelphia, PUT began as an effort to help prisoners with a successful re-entry into the community. PUT worked out of office space donated by Cookman Church. Co-founder Thomas Simms, now executive director, has guided the development of PUT from these small beginnings into a multi-purpose agency that divides its extensive array of programs into four areas:

- Pre-release re-entry programs, including seminars and workshops by ex-offenders and professionals, family support services, help with probation and parole, and housing assistance for male and female prisoners in all prisons throughout the county.

- Post-release programs, offering substance abuse recovery referrals, offender support groups, family support services, community service projects, and other services. In 1997, PUT opened Jefferson House, a transitional house for male ex-offenders, and has plans to open another one.

- The youth self-empowerment program, funded by the local Department of Human Services, an after-school project providing for at-risk youth assistance with computers, tutoring, journal writing, cultural workshops, sports, and other activities.

- Community partnership, in which PUT and its members have become key community resources through building a local park, offering community service by offenders, and providing security for local events and an escort service for senior citizens. PUT is also involved in a cooperative arrangement with its office space partner, Riverside Care, Inc., which offers outpatient drug treatment.

In exploring the secret of PUT's success, putting down roots in a specific local neighborhood and continuity of leadership and support surely must be among the factors that have made it work. Its strong connection to the community in north central Philadelphia and the consistency of direction from Thomas Simms, Rev. Hynicka (still on the board of directors), and others, give it the sort of integrity and solidity necessary to survive and flourish in an arena where start-ups and failures among non-profits are legion. It is also likely that PUT's practice of staffing itself primarily with ex-offenders and persons in recovery gives it the kind of wisdom and legitimacy required to thrive in this field.

5. Georgia: Crime Victims Advocacy Council. (CVAC) began under the auspices of the North Georgia Conference of the United Methodist Church in 1989, later becoming a separate organization. Directed by a professional counselor, CVAC serves metropolitan Atlanta with programs geared toward victims of crime, especially those who are typically underserved by other agencies for victim advocacy.

In addition to working closely with other local agencies such as rape crisis centers, domestic violence task forces, and child abuse councils, CVAC also offers its own programs, including the following:

- Crisis intervention—by phone, at hospitals, and in home visits

- Annual community-wide memorial services for murder victims' families

- Peer support groups for crime victims, organized and run by trained volunteers

- Assistance in filing for victim compensation from the state

- Educational programs and seminars about the criminal justice system and victims' issues

- Personal advocacy and service—e.g., babysitting, accompaniment to court, transportation, etc.

- A large database for referrals to helping agencies throughout Georgia

- Individual counseling

Homicide-surviving family members attend an annual memorial service at Northside UMC in Atlanta, sponsored by CVAC

In recent years, CVAC has expanded to include a pastoral care division that addresses the spiritual and theological concerns of many crime victims. Rev. Bruce Cook, co-founder of CVAC, is head of the new division. A retired federal prison chaplain, he knows the offender side of crime. And he knows the victim side—all too well. In the late 1970s his stepbrother was beaten to death, and he has been a passionate advocate for victims' and survivors' rights and needs ever since.

As CVAC's chaplain, Cook, together with seminary interns, offers pastoral counseling, healing services, Disciple Bible studies, prayer vigils, funeral services, and death notifications for crime victims who need not only personal support and professional therapy, but also an explicitly spiritual intervention or response. In the past, Cook has also been instrumental in moving the state legislature to enact more victim-friendly legislation.

Bruce Cook is a strong voice for a more rehabilitative and redemptive approach to prison programming and for a criminal justice system that is more sensitive and empowering to crime victims. He points to CVAC as one of only three United Methodist-related ministries with crime victims in the country, and feels strongly that this must change if we are to take Jesus' Parable of the Good Samaritan as seriously as we do the Parable of the Last Judgment.

6. *California: Buff and Cindy Whitman-Bradley.* Buff and Cindy Whitman-Bradley live in Marin County, California, and have a passion for restorative justice. Presently in training to become family mediators, they do volunteer work for the Prison Activist Resource Center in Oakland. Each week they visit both Rudolph Roybal on death row at San Quentin prison, and a woman at the federal prison in Dublin. They are also seeking contact with United Methodists and others in South Dakota to help work for criminal justice reform in the area around the Pine Ridge reservation, where relatives of their friend at Dublin live and suffer under a racist and ineffective system.

Cindy and Buff are members of First United Methodist EarthChurch in San Rafael, California, and in 2001 drafted the resolution "Prisons and Restorative Justice," which, with the help of the local chapter of the Methodist Federation for Social Action, was passed by the California-Nevada Annual Conference. One of the things this resolution does is to create a restorative justice task force, under the auspices of the conference Board of Church and Society, that can become a vehicle which Buff, Cindy, and others called to prison and restorative justice ministries can use to spread the word and find allies in the conference.

7. *Tennessee: Mediation and Restitution Reconciliation Services (MARRS)*. Located in Christ United Methodist Church, Memphis, MARRS provides free mediation services for victims and first- and second-time juvenile property offenders in cases referred by the Shelby County juvenile court. Each case is co-mediated by two trained volunteers, usually in a school, community center, or church in the victim's (and often the offender's) neighborhood. In most cases, victims and offenders reach an agreement that both can live with. It often includes probation for the offender, depending on completion of community service that provides restitution to the community as secondary victim. There may also be some form of financial restitution to the primary victim, or uncompensated work at the victim's place of business. Frequently the offense is some form of vandalism. In many cases, the offender's parents are included in the mediation session with the offender and the victim. MARRS monitors the offender's compliance with restitution agreements and then reports the completed case to the court, which then takes no further action.

MARRS was begun in 1993 in partnership not only with the local juvenile court and Christ United Methodist Church, but also with the Memphis Leadership Foundation, a Christian group dedicated to empowerment of Memphis's poor. Funding comes from foundations, individuals, churches, and businesses. No government funding is used. The rate of referred cases with mediation is relatively high, as is the rate of compliance with agreements on the part of offenders. The program's rate of recidivism is low.

Part of MARRS' success may be because it connects many juveniles with positive neighborhood organization such as Boys' Club, Girls' Club, YMCA, athletics, or tutoring programs, and local church youth groups. MARRS stipulates that this be voluntary on the part of the offender. MARRS also operates a community outreach program through which it continues to work with some of the offenders after their cases are closed. This is to "expose at-risk youth from the mediation and truancy programs to Christian principles and examples." Some of these opportunities include after-school activities, Bible study, mentoring, and camps.

8. *Ohio: Good Things Are Happening in Youngstown*. Like many other cities in what is now called the Rust Belt, Youngstown lost its once-thriving steel mills in the late 1970s and began a long downhill slide. During the late 1990s, Youngstown, desperate for new industry and an expanded tax base, sought to acquire new prisons, and now has one of the densest clusters in the United States. The local government made an ill-considered agreement with the Corrections Corporation of America (CCA), resulting in a large new prison. Unbeknownst to local government authorities, the prison was filled with violent, high-security prisoners from Washington, D.C. A rash of killings in and escapes from the prison—

as well as the resulting lawsuits—earned the scorn of local officials and the courts. In 2001, CCA closed the prison. Youngstown, meanwhile, still suffers from serious poverty, a bankrupt public school system, a high rate of violent crime, and a lack of good jobs.

However, some good things are happening. Longtime labor organizers and lawyers Staughton and Alice Lynd live there and work with unions—including one prison guards' union—to gain more power and equality for working people. They also work with prisoners in the area, seeking to help build coalitions between prisoners' self-help groups and progressive working-class and anti-racist groups on the outside. Such work is both promising and immensely frustrating. Equally so is the street-level, day-to-day work of compassion and empowerment with troubled and at-risk members of the next generation, low-income children and youth—and their families. This is the kind of work done by Youngstown's United Methodist Community Center—as well as many other similar centers throughout the country. Among the services offered are the following:

■ A home-based case management service

■ Outreach to juvenile felony offenders (ages 10 to 18) returning to the community from state institutions

■ Nine family-readiness centers in local schools

■ A truancy intervention program for 160 families with children in grades K-8

■ Stoplift, a retail thrift school for shoplifters in five counties

■ A program for females ages 12 to 22 who are locked up, on probation, or on parole

■ An after-school program at three sites, one at the center and two in housing projects

■ A mentoring program

■ A family-stability program as an alternative to out-of-home placement of children

■ A monthly focus group for parents

All program services at the United Methodist Community Center include a minimum sixty days of follow-up and aftercare. It is not beyond the realm of possibility that this center in Youngstown has prevented more crime than all the jails and prisons in Ohio put together. And not by punishing people.

9. Nationwide: JustPeace. This program grew out of several persons' deep concern about conflict resolution. Mary Logan, former general counsel for The United Methodist Church's General Council on Finance and Administration (GCFA), spent most of her professional time with issues of conflict within the church. She is acutely aware of the contradictions between the gospel of reconciliation and our church's and our society's practice of addressing conflict in litigious and adversarial ways.

Logan found a crucial ally in Rev. Tom Porter of Boston's Mellick and Porter law firm, for whom the theory and practice of restorative justice were

helping in his personal struggle to be a Christian and a lawyer. Logan and Porter had many conversations about the church's need to handle conflict in this constructive and transforming way. Unexpected funds made it possible to establish a UMC conflict transformation center, and JustPeace was born.

The mission of JustPeace is "to prepare and assist United Methodists to engage conflict constructively in a way that strives for justice, reconciliation, resource preservation, and restoration of community in the church and the world." It does this through training, consultation, resource development, referrals, networking, and education throughout the church. Its newsletter, website, annual gathering for church "peacebuilders," and other tools help it to develop and facilitate relationships, foster a climate for restorative justice, and build competence in conflict transformation within the church by offering concrete help to faith communities within the United Methodist Church and elsewhere. When Porter points to the basis of JustPeace's work, he articulates the work of restorative justice, as well: "The work of mediation and conflict transformation is spiritual work, and must be grounded in a ministry of reconciliation."

10. Tennessee: Visitation on Death Row (VODR). Since Tennessee, like many other states, reinstated the death penalty in 1977, its death row has gradually filled up. In 1992, as the pace of capital sentences picked up, the Tennessee Coalition to Abolish State Killing began its Visitation on Death Row (VODR) program—an effort to find a non-family visitor for every Tennessee prisoner who has been sentenced to death, and who has no

other regular visitor and would like a VODR friend.

Since early 1993, a VODR training team has recruited and trained approximately 100 persons, mostly from area churches. About 50 of those persons are presently visiting the men and women on death row with whom they were paired. The others have either decided not to visit, moved out of town, been unable to "click" with their prisoners, or seen them transferred to other prisons after having their death sentences changed to life. Some visitors have testified in new trials or new sentencing hearings and been of assistance in winning life sentences for their friends instead of death.

VODR trainers, who have all made death row visits for years, offer individual support and consultation to newer visitors. VODR visitors also get together every few months, with whoever wishes to participate, in the private dining room of a local restaurant to swap stories, share experiences, and get support for what can be very difficult work. VODR may be the most extensive death row visitation program in the United States.

11. Minnesota: Strong Commitment to Restorative Justice. Minnesota leads all states in the United States in its commitment to restorative justice. In 1993, after a series of conferences, studies, and public opinion surveys, the state's Department of Corrections hired Kay Pranis as its first full-time restorative justice planner. Pranis and her colleagues began their work with a broad educational campaign throughout the state on the philosophy and values of restorative justice. They provided strategic consultation and technical assistance in exploring, designing, and carrying out ways of applying restorative justice principles, a process that continues to this day. Pranis's office also creates networks of professionals and community activists for mutual support and sharing of information.

The results have been anything but standardized cookie-cutter programs. Pranis and the Department of Corrections believe in the importance of context, flexibility, community control, and experimentation, so they function as guides and consultants, not as dictators. Many communities and agencies do different things, all from a restorative justice perspective and informed by restorative justice values. Some examples:

- Victim-offender mediation and dialogue in a number of counties and prisons

- Family-group conferencing by schools, human services, churches, community programs, law enforcement, courts, and probation offices—and, in one women's prison, for inmate disputes

- Community panels for diversion and probation of offenders in such venues as Walker Community United Methodist Church in the Powderhorn Park community of South Minneapolis

- Circle sentencing and peacemaking circles on Native American reservations, the Twin Cities, and rural areas

- Meaningful community service projects in many counties and at several institutions

- Victim impact panels and victim empathy classes in a number of counties and at several prisons

- Peer mediation programs in many schools throughout the state

The Minnesota experience in learning and practicing restorative justice has, by all accounts, been rich and fruitful. It is an example of a government-community partnership in which the state has played the essential role of articulating and legitimizing a central vision and undergirding the work of local groups in a variety of ways.

Minnesota is one of the few examples of successful, intentional, progressive change in a state's approach to the problems of crime and justice. It shows what is possible when an exciting vision is combined with political courage; strategic preparation; a gifted leader; and a wise, respectful, flexible, supportive process.

12. *Texas: Restorative Justice Ministries Network (RJMN) and Texas Impact.* At the beginning of the new millennium, Texas looked like the least likely place for movement in progressive, humane, criminal justice reform. Record rates of execution, an indigent defense system that is itself criminal, a huge and rapidly growing rate of incarceration, wholesale adoption of private for-profit prisons, politician-judges bought and paid for by the highest bidder—all this, and a governor running for president on a tough-on-crime platform. But now that Bush is president, and no longer governor, the Texas legislature is showing signs of moving into the modern world. Things are changing.

Although few progressive criminal justice bills were actually passed and signed by the new governor, there was significant legislative action in 2001 concerning a number of important issues: hate crimes, indigent defense, a moratorium on executions, life without parole as a sentencing alternative to the death penalty, and exempting the mentally retarded from the death penalty. Suddenly, in 2001, even privatization of prisons and growth in the rate of incarceration are no longer inviolate.

Perhaps one of the responsible factors is the steadily developing Restorative Justice Ministries Network (RJMN) in Texas, a collection of traditional prison ministry professionals and volunteers brought together by a restorative justice-oriented leader, Rev. Emmett Solomon. RJMN is Baptist-dominated, theologically evangelical in flavor, and politically conservative. However, that which is evangelical and politically conservative can still have a progressive effect on criminal justice if the leadership knows the territory, which Solomon—a retired Texas prison chaplain—does. But if the Texas legislature continues the new trend, much of the credit must go to a scrappy, grassroots—but professional—interfaith group called Texas Impact.

Texas Impact is working hard and effectively to change public policy and practice in criminal justice as well as in other areas of state government. Headed by Bee Moorhead, a former state government employee, the organization is heavily dependent on United Methodists for much its membership, volunteer support, and funding. Over a fourth of Texas Impact's individual members are United Methodists, many of them United Methodist Women, and roughly a third of its board members are Methodists. Each year, Texas Impact's legislative training event for the Texas United Methodist Women is a major event. According to Moorhead, "Texas Impact couples its efforts to educate activists on the legislative process and issue advocacy with a commitment to bringing religious activists and elected officials into dialogue. We work with bill sponsors on bill language, line up testimony, and schedule events such as legislative breakfasts where clergy can meet legislators. We help our members develop ongoing relationships with lawmakers so that they can make quick, effective contact when bills are in committee."

Texas Impact is convinced that members of the United Methodist Church and other faith communities in Texas have the potential to bring about positive change in Texas's justice system. But its surveys find that, like members of other churches, many United Methodists are unaware of the denomination's positions on social and criminal justice issues and are begging for help and leadership from their church in assessing and acting on these issues. To meet this need, Texas Impact is developing a five-part study curriculum, "Texas Faith Looks at Texas Justice," which looks at Texas's criminal justice policies and practices from a Judeo-Christian perspective. It is designed for United Methodist Women groups, Sunday classes, Wednesday night meetings, and their equivalents in other denominations. Its first installment on the death penalty has been very popular.

13. *Michigan: Much Good Work in Kalamazoo and Beyond.* In Kalamazoo, Michigan, and beyond, much is happening in the area of restorative justice. Both in Kalamazoo County and in Paw Paw, county seat of the neighboring county, Van Buren, there are some extraordinary judges. Judge William Buhl, a Presbyterian layman, routinely makes creative, humane, and restorative rulings and sentences that take seriously the community's public safety, the victims, the law, and the offender. His approach and his decisions are accepted by

the small community of Paw Paw because he is not only personable, but well-rooted and respected in the community. Judge William Schma of Kalamazoo, a leader in the national movement of therapeutic jurisprudence (very close to restorative justice in values and language), is equally forthright in his insistence that criminal court judges need to be a kind of social worker. He believes that because so many offenders have mental health and substance abuse problems, any other judicial approach would be morally irresponsible as well as ineffective.

The Kalamazoo community and the churches in both counties have networked well with each other and have a variety of restorative justice-oriented programs in place, including an ecumenical prison ministry and an after-care program.

Camp New Day for children with imprisoned parents—
located in Camp Albright, Michigan

A dispute resolution group provides mediation of cases referred by courts, schools, and businesses in five counties. Programs in Kalamazoo County deal with such matters as drug-court diversion, probation enhancement, and support for battered women. The Kalamazoo Coalition for Youth Violence Prevention has taken the initiative to bring these and other groups together in order to create a broadly based network to produce, fund,

and staff a county plan for restorative justice.

Justus House, located in Lane Boulevard United Methodist Church, in a multi-ethnic working-class neighborhood of Kalamazoo, and functioning since 1995, "serves the community by providing a healing ministry and practical assistance to victims, released prisoners, and their families in Kalamazoo and Van Buren counties," in the words of its brochure. It helps with counseling, employment assistance, referrals to recovery programs, and support groups for parents and victims. Furthermore, Chuck Wilson, a United Methodist layman, is negotiating with the Kalamazoo school system to develop more restorative justice possibilities in local schools.

14. *Tennessee: Outreach Penal After Care Empowerment (PACE)*. Harold G. Bryson is a member of Stanley United Methodist Church in Chattanooga, Tennessee. Since 1996, operating out of a previously vacant building on his church's grounds, he has offered newly released prisoners hospitality, transportation, and referrals to community agencies. As director of W.S. Hight Community Outreach Penal After Care Empowerment (PACE), Harold Bryson's real goal—and that of his volunteer colleagues—is " to assist individuals with their most urgent need so that they may make a positive transition from incarceration to a crime-free and prison-free lifestyle."

The Hight/PACE board of directors is composed largely of clergy and laypersons from the Stanley United Methodist Church, but also has Baptist representation. A distinctly grassroots program, PACE is based primarily within the African American community. It has good working relationships with the local jail, workhouse, and other criminal justice agencies, but its real mission is to develop relationships—at a very critical time—with men and women released from prison, with little money, few friends, and sometimes no family support.

Like many community- and congregation-based ministries in the criminal justice arena, PACE operates with very limited funds. Meanwhile, Bryson and his friends continue to meet and walk with their neighbors—often forgotten and despised men and women at one of the most crucial times in their lives.

15. *Oregon: Oregon Criminal Justice Reform Coalition; Western Prison Project; SAFES.* Several women in Portland, Oregon, are determined to make restorative justice a reality in their state and in a seven-state region in the West. Brigette Sarabi is a former foundation program officer who had a family member imprisoned on a drug charge. She is drawing on both her job skills and her personal experience to organize a regional grassroots campaign for criminal justice reform in western United States. Brigette's friend Arwen Bird had an even more devastating experience. She was the designated driver for a carload of friends (including her sister) which was struck by a car driven by an intoxicated young man. The result? Arwen is partially paralyzed and wheelchair-bound, and her sister continues to struggle with brain damage caused by a head injury. But don't call Arwen a victim. She and fellow members of SAFES (see below) are survivors.

Brigette Sarabi directs the Oregon Criminal Justice Reform Coalition. This group, in 2001, was instrumental in forging an unlikely coalition of prisoners' rights advocates, prisoners and their families, correctional officers' unions, and crime victims that persuaded the state legislature to restore $9 million in state funds for prisoner rehabilitation and treatment programs. Now she leads the effort to develop a regional coalition of citizens' action groups in Oregon, Washington, Idaho, Montana, Utah, Wyoming, and Nevada. When the Western Prison Project (WPP) held its founding convention in spring 2001, it agreed to make restorative justice central to its mission statement.

The Western Prison Project has already written and published a groundbreaking study, *The Prison Payoff: The Role of Politics and Private Prisons in the Incarceration Boom.* Among other things, this book exposes the role of the American Legislative Exchange Council—dominated by executives of private for-profit prison companies and conservative state legislators—in drafting and lobbying for "model criminal justice legislation" in state legislatures all over the United States. But the WPP is just getting started.

One of the most dynamic groups in WPP is SAFES (Survivors Advocating for an Effective System), founded in 1999 by Arwen Bird, the young woman who was paralyzed in a car accident. The cover of SAFES's brochure reads, "'Our vision is a safer and more humane Oregon. Oregon's justice system is based on vengeance. We believe it should be based on what works." Arwen Bird continues her analysis: "Most of the people spouting 'get tough on crime' rhetoric aim to speak for us. They don't! We disagree with the death penalty, mandatory minimum sentences, rampant prison construction and all the other planks of a criminal justice philosophy motivated by revenge and profit. We favor prevention, rehabilitation and restitution. We favor positive action over emotional and political reaction."

With a strong track record of education, advocacy, and community organizing for such a young group, SAFES is now receiving the help of WPP in building its organizational capacity and in expanding its work into the seven-state area. As it continues to grow, SAFES could become a much-needed model for strong, progressive victims'/survivors' rights organizations. Nothing is more important for promoting a truly restorative approach to criminal justice in the United States.

16. *Iowa: A Range of Restorative Justice Ministries.* When the General Board of Global Ministries' new office for restorative justice ministries in Bloomington, Minnesota, held its first event in September 1999, Beje Clark, a former Iowa Republican state legislator and the Iowa Annual Conference's restorative justice advocate, had doctor's orders not to travel. But not to worry: As proof of Clark's effectiveness, the conference sent a delegation of nine people who called themselves "The Bloomington Nine."

The restorative justice committee of which they are a part, includes representatives from the Board of Church and Society, United Methodist Women, Commission on the Status and Role of Women, Board of Global Ministries, Missions Committee, Board of Laity, Christian Unity, the Christian Educators Fellowship, a district council on ministries, and the conference staff. Under Beje Clark's leadership, restorative justice task forces have been set up in seventeen of Iowa's ninety-nine mostly rural counties, and the Iowa conference's resolution supporting restorative justice

has been on the books since 1993, and was reaffirmed in 1999.

The committee's new chairperson, Jean Basinger of Des Moines, is active in a number of other United Methodist and ecumenical criminal justice ministry initiatives as well. They include the following:

- The Iowa office of CURE (Citizens United for the Rehabilitation of Errants), which works for prison reform and offers support for families and friends of prisoners

- Criminal Justice Ministries, which operates Hospitality House for male ex-prisoners, a prison pen pals program, the *Bars and Stripes* newsletter, and an advocacy ministry

- Knight's House, for women coming out of prison

- Trinity United Methodist Church's prison van ministry, which takes families and friends to prisons to visit their loved ones

Des Moines is also the site of an innovative program for local citizens charged with welfare fraud, unemployment fraud, and other selected misdemeanors. Qualifying defendants are given the option of pleading guilty to a lesser charge; paying restitution under the Polk County attorney's supervision; and participating in an intense, one-day, adult life-skills program held at Immanuel United Methodist Church. There members of Immanuel and of three other neighborhood churches (Lutheran, Catholic, and Presbyterian) offer hospitality and a home-cooked meal. Staff from a non-profit community agency conduct the class, which covers such issues as managing stress, anger, and conflict; financial management; finding help for addiction recovery; and other life skills. Over lunch, pleas are accepted and sentences of restitution are imposed by a judge. Most persons who meet the terms of their agreement can later have the other parts of their sentence deferred and/or their record expunged. The assistant county prosecutor who oversees the program, credits the church's hospitality as a factor in the success of the program, which has a very high rate of restitution compliance, and a recidivism rate of less than one percent.

Another part of the Iowa conference's ministry of restorative justice was directed by Carlos Jayne, its legislative advocate until his recent retirement. Jayne, and United Methodists working with him, pushed the state legislature toward action on bills consistent with the United Methodist Social Principles, General Conference resolutions, and Iowa Annual Conference resolutions—like its restorative justice statement. Several years ago, United Methodists were instrumental in defeating a bill that would have brought the death penalty back to Iowa—one of only twelve states without it. Lana Ross is the newly appointed legislative advocate.

Other annual conferences in the United Methodist Church might consider looking to Iowa for guidance, not only in its pioneering work in prison ministry and in promoting restorative justice as an alternative to a retributive justice system, but also for its coupling of discipleship and citizenship in the legislative advocacy program. The restorative justice committee, the legislative advocacy program—these and other structures give "legs" to Beje Clark's comment, citing

2 Corinthians 5:17-20, when she reminds us that churches are called to the ministry of healing relationships: "Anyone in Christ is a new creation. God has given us the ministry of reconciliation."

17. *Virginia: Conflict Transformation Program, Eastern Mennonite University.* In this study book we have looked at restorative justice as an alternative approach in the area of criminal justice. Another way to see restorative justice is as one dimension of a larger conceptual paradigm shift— and social movement—in the wide arena of social conflict. This is how it is understood at Eastern Mennonite University in Harrisonburg, Virginia. EMU's Conflict Transformation Program, begun in 1993, is rooted in the Anabaptist, peace church version of Christian theology and practice, today most commonly represented by the Mennonites. In its own language, "the program is designed to support the personal and professional development of individuals as peace builders and to strengthen the peace building and restorative justice capacities of the institutions they serve."

According to Carolyn Schrock-Schenk, director of the Mennonite Conciliation Service, there are three basic elements in any conflict: problem, process, people. Conflict transformation is a move away from "conflict resolution" and "conflict management"—in which problem and process, respectively, are central—to a strategy more directly focused on the people in conflict and their relationships with one another. Transforming conflict requires confronting or intervening in it in order to change its dynamics, so peace can be built between those in conflict. The CTP believes that effective conflict transformation "must address root causes of conflict, must be developed strategically, and must promote healing of relationships and restoration of the torn fabric of the human community." EMU's Conflict Transformation Program deals with all sorts of conflicts—between nations; between ethnic or religious groups within nations; between crime victims and victimizers; and so on. The curriculum's restorative justice dimension is led by Howard Zehr, author of the seminal book *Changing Lenses*, and possibly the foremost pioneer among restorative justice practitioners and

Participants in Conflict Transformation Program

theoreticians in the United States.

EMU's Conflict Transformation Program has the following components:

- The master of arts degree, with full- and limited-residency formats

- The Summer Peace-Building Institute, offering intensive week-long courses in specialized aspects of peace building to more than 150 participants from more than forty countries

- The Institute for Justice and Peace-building, CTP's applied practice-and-research component, which offers culturally contextualized training and consultant work with partners throughout the world

All feature a wide and diverse global spectrum of cultures, nations, academic disciplines, and professional vocations among faculty, students, and clients. For exploration of and education in the deeper and wider ranges of restorative justice and its larger field of conflict engagement and transformation, this Mennonite school in the middle of Virginia's Shenandoah Valley—ironically, rich in Revolutionary and Civil War history—may be one of the best places to go.

18. *Nationwide: The Journey of Hope ... From Violence to Healing.* This is an educational and awareness tour that spreads the message of forgiveness. It began as a project of Murder Victims' Families for Reconciliation (MFVR), but became a separate organization in the late 1990s. The Journey of Hope is led by murder victims' family members who share their stories about the process of healing through reconciliation. Calling for alternatives to the death penalty, they are joined by families of death row prisoners, death row survivors, and friends and activists from around the world. Their message provides a stunning picture of the cycle of violence and the way in which the death penalty prevents healing, prolongs suffering, and creates more victims.

Every year, the Journey conducts an intensive two-week tour of a different state. Its members travel in the host state, speaking to high-school and college classes, churches, synagogues, mosques, other community organizations, and the media. Their message of hope and forgiveness offers a powerful alternative to the voices of vengeance and the many images of violence.

The Journey of Hope . . . from Violence to Healing is an important opportunity to be at the very heart of restorative justice with deeply concerned people who give up their vacations each year to tell—over and over again, to hundreds of strangers—the story of the worst thing that ever happened to them. It is community education, public advocacy, and restorative justice, all in one.

19. *Georgia: Prison and Jail Project.* The combination of old-fashioned racism, poverty, and punishment probably doesn't get much worse than in

Smithville. The founder of the Prison and Jail Project, John Cole Vodicka, and his work partner, Elizabeth Dede, each have a long history of working with love and for justice in the deep South.

Cole Vodicka discovered the American South's criminal injustice system when he was imprisoned during the Vietnam War for draft resistance. He has been fighting that system—nonviolently—

Freedomwalk 2001 rally at Dawson, Georgia Youth Community Center

many of the thirty-three counties that make up southwest Georgia. The region includes Albany, where a courageous civil rights movement was thwarted in the 1960s, and Plains, the hometown of former president Jimmy Carter. Just down the road is Americus, the home of Habitat for Humanity. It is in Americus where, in 1942, radical Baptist preacher/farmer Clarence Jordan and others started Koinonia Farm to practice Christian communism, Christian pacifism, and Christian interracial community. But today the edgiest, most risky thing happening in this area may well be the work of the Prison and Jail Project, based in Americus with branch offices in Dawson and

ever since. During the 1970s and 1980s he worked in Louisiana and South Carolina with the Southern Coalition on Jails and Prisons (a regional movement for prisoners' rights), a moratorium on prison building, alternatives to incarceration, and an end to the death penalty. After several years of running Alderson Hospitality House near a federal women's prison in West Virginia, he and his family moved into the Koinonia community in the late 1980s. Cole Vodicka began a jail and prison ministry/advocacy project there, and later spun it off to become the Prison and Jail Project. Dede recently joined him in this work, after many years of living and working with homeless and death-row persons while in residence as a partner at the Open Door, a "Presbyterian Catholic Worker" community in Atlanta. John Cole Vodicka and his family, and Elizabeth Dede, are members of Oakhurst Presbyterian Church in Atlanta, which serves as the Prison and Jail Project's financial sponsor.

Georgia's incarceration rate is in the top five of all states, and in southwest Georgia alone, 40,000 men, women, and children—most of them poor and African American—are currently in jail or prison, or on parole or probation. The state ranks fiftieth in the nation in providing funding for the defense of indigent persons charged with crimes. At the risk of their own freedom, their safety, and possibly their lives, Cole Vodicka, Dede, and their mostly African American colleagues and volunteers work within this environment in a very basic but strategically sophisticated way, to minister, educate, advocate, organize, empower, and litigate around issues of juvenile and criminal justice in their region. They have gone to jail a few times themselves and have had their newsletter censored by prison officials, but they continue to grow and to win victories even in such a hostile climate.

Each September the staff, volunteers, constituents, and other friends spend a week on a "Freedomwalk" through some of the region's counties, calling attention to unjust jail, prison, and courthouse conditions and practices as they journey from town to town. They also lift up unheralded local heroes and martyrs from the days of the civil rights struggle and from more recent—even current—times A byproduct of these walks is a focus on local historical educa-

tion with and for each other, as well as through the media.

As they say every two months in Freedomways, they are working "to build a coalition of people—imprisoned and free—who can begin to speak out for change in the system and for justice." How do they define that justice? Well, it's "a justice that is healing, reconciling, and transformative." If this vision of what the United Methodist Church would call restorative justice can even be envisioned, even be dreamed about, in the racist and oppressive cauldron of southwest Georgia, perhaps it can happen anywhere.

20. *Alabama: Radical Discipleship in Downtown Birmingham.* The Church of the Reconciler does not have restorative justice programs *per se.* But because the church is situated where it is, because its members are who they are, and because of the gospel the congregation has committed itself to, pastor and members are engaged every day in doing restorative justice. Formed in the last years of the twentieth century as an intentionally multiracial, multi-class, diversity-embracing congregation in downtown Birmingham, it is trying to embody for its time and place the radical discipleship of the first-century church.

Within a historical and geographical context of vicious racism and grinding poverty, this is one congregation that "walks the walk" as well as "talks the talk" of Christian faith. A mix of black, white, and brown; of affluent and poor; of gay and straight; of young and old, the church reflects and blends in with its neighborhood, but in a way that marks it clearly as an alternative community dedicated to a way of life distinctively and radically

Christian. Rev. R. Lawton Higgs Sr., pastor of the Church of the Reconciler, echoes the vision of biblical Jubilee justice when he proclaims that "God's work is the work of removing the injustices of the past that divide and limit all of us."

This church embraces both worship and mission, rejects addiction but embraces (not enables) its many addicts to support their recovery, and feeds the many hungry—physically and spiritually—in the congregation and its immediate neighborhood. Radical hospitality is offered to all. There are weekly Bible studies for all ages, a school for urban Christian living, hot lunches for all, a clothes closet, field trips for children, and occasional weekend workshops for adults on such topics as welfare reform, homosexuality and the church, and living in a violent society. The church's brochure summarizes Christian life in community: "Everyone is welcome with their own fear and prejudice to become part of the healing and reconciling process. The workload is high, and the tangible results of worldly success are few and far between. But the fruits of peace and justice are there."

For Lawton Higgs and others in the congregation, a big part of this workload is a very hands-on restorative justice ministry: binding up the wounds of the violated; getting people out of jail; mediating conflicts between homeless men and women; providing support and referral services for the addicted; and advocating for changes in the criminal justice system, including an end to the death penalty in Alabama. The experience of the Church of the Reconciler reminds us that—like Christian discipleship—the ministry of restorative justice is not primarily a matter of committees and programs, but of being the church, in the right place, with the right heart, and made up of all God's people.

21. *Maine: Maine Council of Churches Develops Climate for Restorative Justice.* The Maine Council of Churches (MCC) must be serious about restorative justice. For a number of years, under the successive leadership of restorative justice advocates like Russ Immarigeon, Evelyn Hanneman, and now Suzanne Rudalevige, the council has helped to develop a climate throughout the state that is increasingly open to restorative justice policies and practices. Rudalevige, a United Methodist and a former practicing lawyer, has for years provided leadership in criminal and restorative justice for the New England conference. Her current ecumenical work with the MCC takes her into faith communities, the state legislature, juvenile and criminal justice agencies, prisons, and schools throughout the state as she educates, advocates, and organizes for restorative justice principles, values, processes, and programs. Recent and current initiatives include the following:

- Organizing interfaith workshops about ministry with crime victims

- Helping develop community resolution teams

enabling nonviolent juvenile offenders and their victims to work out settlements without the courts

- Observing Restorative Justice Week with an awards banquet and a publication highlighting state and other restorative justice projects

- Monitoring criminal justice legislation and testifying from a restorative justice perspective in public hearings in the state legislature

- Working with other groups for restorative discipline in schools; better mental health services in prisons and jails; reintegration programs for released prisoners; gender-specific programs for girls in the juvenile justice system; and police and service agency collaboration to break the cycle of arrest/court/jail for the mentally ill and drug-addicted

The work of the Maine Council of Churches and others in the state has led the state's Department of Corrections to adopt restorative justice as one of its guiding principles. Communities throughout the state are exploring and developing a variety of restorative and progressive initiatives. A hint for those in other states: The Maine Council of Churches' ongoing, effective work with restorative justice over a lengthy period shows what can be done by a statewide ecumenical or interfaith organization committed to enlisting communities of faith in the work of criminal justice ministries and reform. Such a coalition can function with a degree of

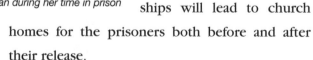
Art created by a woman during her time in prison

breadth, depth, and continuity that is difficult to create or sustain by any one denomination or congregation.

22. *North Carolina: In the Footsteps of John Wesley.* Rev. Jerry Murray of the Western North Carolina Conference got hooked on prison ministry long ago. He knows everything there is to know about John and Charles Wesley's ministry to prisoners, beginning with the Oxford years. To hear Murray talk about his own experiences and feelings, you almost think you are listening to John Wesley himself. In North Carolina, Murray established and nourished an extensive network of ecumenical Yokefellow groups in the state's prisons. For many years he was engaged in a wide-ranging speaking/preaching/consulting/recruiting ministry to spread the gospel to the imprisoned and their friends.

Now that Murray is retired, he and Rev. Mark Hicks of the Western North Carolina conference and others are establishing Disciple Bible Study groups in as many of North Carolina's eighty-six prisons as possible, as well as in United Methodist congregations near those prisons. It is their hope that participation in these groups will create contact between church people and prisoners—and that these relationships will lead to church homes for the prisoners both before and after their release.

It all started in 1995, when a recent group of Disciple Bible Study graduates at Mt. Pisgah United Methodist Church in Greensboro contacted a minister at a prison in Winston-Salem with the idea of establishing a group to do the study there. The first group graduated in May 1996, three more groups began in September of that year, and it's been growing ever since, with much support from leaders of the state's Department of Corrections and the bishops of both annual conferences.

The various projects profiled so far only scratch the surface of the healing, restorative way in which many United Methodists and others work in the crime and justice arena throughout the nation. We conclude this chapter with the briefest acknowledgments of a range of such ministries. Some are personal and individual, or they are special projects that small groups of United Methodists do on their own. Others are ecumenical or government programs in which United Methodists do volunteer or staff work. Or they are special initiatives of denominational agencies, individual bishops, or annual conferences. All grow out of a vision of *shalom*, a compassionate heart, and a spirit of discipleship.

■ A new unit of United Methodist Women was begun at the Pennsylvania State Correctional Institution for Women in Muncy, in the Central Pennsylvania Annual Conference.

■ Maxine Bromfield and other members of Crawford Memorial United Methodist Women in the Bronx, New York, visit women at a women's prison in Bedford Hills, New York, and work with their children.

■ The Women's Division and the Minnesota Annual Conference provide significant funding for the Minneapolis-based Center for Victims of Torture.

■ United Methodist Women of the Kansas East Annual Conference sponsor weekend retreats for women prisoners and their children, and arrange parenting classes for male and female prisoners.

■ The United Methodist Neighborhood Center of Utica, New York, started an alternative-to-incarceration program for mentally ill adults that was later taken over by the state. The center still helps its neighbors and clients with addiction problems, domestic violence, and nonviolent conflict resolution.

■ Los Duros (The Tough Ones), the United Methodist Houchens Community Center's program for Latino youth, and its Mujeres Fuertes (Women with Power) program for young Latina mothers offer athletic activities, exposure to spiritual discipline, tutoring, conflict resolution, and alternatives to gangs in Houchens, New Mexico.

■ Bishop Felton May and Baltimore United Methodist churches are offering addicts in drug-infested neighborhoods the following services: tent "saving stations" with health care, food, clothing, and prayer ministries. They are also putting pressure on the city to offer more beds for drug treatment.

■ Rev. Larry Wayman of Oxnard, California, conducts the Faith Connection, an interfaith ministry with survivors of murder and other violent crime in Ventura County. The ministry holds candlelight vigils for the murdered, works with youth in gangs, and arranges discussions with community groups about effective ways to oppose violence.

■ Rev. Jerry Goebel of the National Hispanic Plan conducts various ministries in Yakima County, Washington, primarily with Hispanic youth in gangs, juvenile detention, or adult jails.

- In 1991, Rev. Louise Stowe Johns started Epiphany Ministry (a Kairos-type intensive 3-day course in Christianity for incarcerated youth) in Alabama. Today, Epiphany Ministry operates in more than ten states. Recently Stowe was instrumental in putting together an effort that resulted in the commuting, by the governor of Alabama, of a young woman's death sentence to life imprisonment, an exceedingly rare occurrence in any U.S. state in the last twenty years.

- United Methodist layman Jeff Hunsaker is a national leader in the Kairos prison ministry movement (now operating in approximately thirty states, Australia, England, and South Africa). Currently, Hunsaker—with substantial input from Jewish and Muslim representatives—runs an interfaith prison program in Ohio.

- In January 2000, during the campaign for the U.S. presidency, Fort Worth Area resident Bishop Joe A. Wilson (now retired) wrote a widely publicized "Open Letter to Texas Governor George W. Bush," a United Methodist, reminding him of the United Methodist Church's historic stand against capital punishment and pleading with him to declare a moratorium on executions in Texas.

- Suzanne Seaton, a United Methodist laywoman, is on staff at JOY! Initiative (Joining with Our Youth), which—under the auspices of the Church Council of Greater Seattle—runs a mentoring program for youth returning to the community from the local juvenile detention center.

- United Methodist laywoman Jody Parks Moxley and four other women visit adult and juvenile female inmates weekly for an hour and a half at the Brevard County, Florida, Supervision Center. According to Moxley, such a "Ministry of Listening" could be done by women from most churches at most county jails, with cooperation from the county sheriff.

- United Methodist laywoman Margaret Palmer has spent sixteen years visiting women imprisoned in the Hillsborough County, Florida, jail system, through a spiritual counseling ministry called CHAT (Come Hide Away and Talk).

- Rev. George Allan Bradley works with an ecumenical volunteer program at the Bexar County Adult Detention Center in San Antonio, Texas. MATCH/PATCH (Mommas/Papas And Their Children) focuses on behavior modification and life/parenting-skills as well as family reconciliation.

- In Fort Worth, Texas, Rev. Tim Boegelin works with PACT (Parents and Children Together), a comprehensive program of support services for prisoners' families in order to prevent imprisonment of future generations.

- United Methodist laywoman Dorothy Yeoman serves as a volunteer in the Chicago area. One of her responsibilities is work with Grace House, a women's halfway house that offers addiction recovery, self-esteem classes, adult basic education, parenting classes, job development, and housing referral services.

- Rev. Nancy Haas, a United Methodist pastor, directs an extensive volunteer jail chaplaincy ministry at the Montgomery County, Ohio, jail. Sponsored by Greater Dayton Christian Connections, it offers programs of material and spiritual support, all staffed by volunteers of many faiths and denominations.

- Murray Batt is a United Methodist layman who chairs the committee of the Texas Annual

Conference Criminal Justice and Mercy Ministries (CJAMM). The committee organizes and promotes ministries with male and female prisoners and their families; re-entry and after-care ministries with ex-offenders; ministries with juvenile offenders; and ministries with staff of the criminal justice system.

■ The Women's Division's Nome (Alaska) Community Center is the epicenter of numerous restorative justice programs: a domestic violence shelter, a juvenile probation diversion program, victim-offender mediation (in the building), and community service supervision.

■ Many United Methodists are involved in the programs for prison ministry of the Central Pennsylvania Annual Conference. A former prison chaplain, Rev. Judith Coleman, directs a residential aftercare facility that deals with drug and alcohol addiction. Her husband, Rev. Larry Coleman, is chaplain of the Dauphin County prison. United Methodist laywoman Jane Russell works with the Yokefellow prison ministry and with Bridge Haven, a prisoner family hospitality ministry in Williamsport. Grace Unlimited, in Milesburg, is headed by Lenore Alexander and works with prisoners and their families, pre- and post-release. Anthony Alexander participates in the seven-church Sojourner Truth United Methodist Group Ministry, which works with ex-prisoners, recovering addicts, and dispossessed and disenfranchised persons who have given up on the church.

■ Through St. Luke's United Methodist Church, Houston, Texas, Rev. Wesley Stevens and Marilyn Stevens coordinate The Newgate Connection, a volunteer service offering hospitality to inmates' families waiting to make visits at the Lucile G. Plane State Jail for Women. When asked why, the Stevenses reply, "We stood where you are standing"—waiting to visit their own daughter when she was imprisoned there.

Other Ways to Respond

One-on-One Visits

Val Hinshaw attended a workshop on prison reform led by Laura Wells approximately twenty-five years ago in Missouri. Val said, "I remember my resistance, thinking, 'Who would want to do that? Oh, well, maybe this is what I'm supposed to do.'" Not long after that, she attended a seminar led by Harold DeWolf. That seminar spoke to her, although she had minimal involvement with prison ministry during the next four or five years. Then she was contacted and asked to become a one-on-one volunteer with a young mother whom we'll call Jerri, who had recently been given a life sentence with the stipulation that she must serve fifty years in prison before she could be considered for parole. She was bitter and angry and not very likeable. Val, the mother of seven young adult children at the time, was asked and accepted the challenge of becoming Jerri's one-on-one volunteer, visiting her in prison. (It was thought that anyone who had brought up seven children could deal with Jerri!) Val was one of several women who had each been matched with a woman in prison. They went regularly to visit the women, bringing food, having Bible study, and developing personal relationships.

Val has continued to visit and write letters to Jerri, though not as frequently as in the beginning. She's seen tremendous changes in Jerri, who has now spent half of her life in prison. Jerri earned her GED and went through a two-year college drafting program. She has been the facilitator of a domestic violence workshop and became a member of the church. Jerri took advantage of every opportunity to learn and grow. When asked why she continued to visit Jerri for twenty years, Val replied, "We became friends—those of us who made those monthly visits. They were women just like us. . . ."

Pen Pals

It is not feasible for everyone to be a one-on-one volunteer with someone in prison. However, there is another way of visiting, and that is to be a pen pal. This is what Helen Ueleke, also from Missouri, began doing approximately twenty years ago with another woman in prison. They have corresponded ever since, and it has been a meaningful outside contact for the woman with whom she was matched.

Hygiene Kits for Women in Prison

"AIM's (Aid to Inmate Mothers) second annual Christmas Box Project was a wonderful success. Through the collaborative efforts of the prison staff and administration at Julia Tutwiler Prison (in Alabama), over 72 hygiene boxes were purchased for the women who were unable to afford personal necessities for the year...." (Excerpt from newsletter)

In most states, women prisoners are responsible for purchasing most of their items of personal hygiene, but do not have the resources. One way of responding is by providing personal hygiene kits. (Be sure to contact the jail or prison before you collect items. There are certain restrictions and guidelines.)

If you are interested in becoming a volunteer visitor or pen pal, or in providing hygiene kits, contact your conference office to see if someone in your conference is working with restorative justice ministries. Or you can contact the chaplain or volunteer coordinator in your prison to learn what the procedures, training, and needs are. There are organizations in some states whose task it is to match volunteers with inmates.

*Can there be
restorative justice
for whole communities,
societies, or nation states
that have been ripped
apart by violence, torture,
and "human evil on a
collective scale?"*

4

RESTORATIVE JUSTICE IN THE GLOBAL CONTEXT

How do I reconcile with the reality that my sister-in-law and niece were raped in their home by rebels searching for me? What remedy exists when you recognize a fellow churchgoer as the attacker who cut off your brother's hands? Can the society rehabilitate, or should it punish, the legions of children—many of them kidnapped and forced into combat—who committed atrocities? How can the country redress such unspeakable crimes?

—Journalist from Sierra Leone after the announcement by U.N. Secretary General Kofi Annan of the formation of a war crimes tribunal for Sierra Leone, 2001

At the 1998 United Methodist Women's Assembly in Orlando, Florida, United Methodist women listened to a powerful witness from one of their own. The entire assembly hall, filled to capacity, sat transfixed as Elmira Sellu, president of United Methodist Women of the Sierra Leone Annual Conference, shared her story—and that of the United Methodist Women of Sierra Leone—throughout the months and years of violence and conflict in their homeland:

I represent the United Methodist Women in Sierra Leone, a small country in West Africa.

My country has for the past seven years faced many political and socio-economic problems. In 1991, a senseless rebel war broke out as a spill-over from the war in Liberia.

After a brief period of peace and tranquility, and signs of economic growth and development, Sierra Leone was once more plunged into a state of anarchy on the twenty-fifth of May last year [1997]. Our army and the rebels allied themselves and overthrew the legitimate civilian government. For nine months, my country witnessed one of the most barbaric of all coups Africa had ever witnessed.

Apart from the massive looting and burning of both private and public property, women and children were killed, cut in pieces and displayed in street corners. Pregnant women had their stomachs ripped open and fetuses removed. Suckling mothers were forced to kill their babies, pound them in mortars to make ground meat for the rebels to eat. Male children were forced to have sexual intercourse with their mothers and grandmothers in the presence of rebels. School children had both hands cut off. Some, as usual, were recruited to serve as child soldiers and sex workers.

By the grace of God, many like my family and I had cause to flee our country and for the past nine months lived as refugees in neighboring Guinea. Some of our United Methodist fleeing women, living in the towns and in the refugee camps,

lived under subhuman conditions where our young children were plagued with many diseases.

As we reflect upon the testimony of Elmira Sellu and hundreds of thousands of women, men, children, and youth around the globe who have suffered injustice, who have been violated, abused, tortured, and murdered, how can we speak to the questions asked by restorative justice: Who was harmed? What are their needs? Whose obligation are they?

Can there be restorative justice for whole communities, societies, or nation-states that have been ripped apart by poverty, violence, torture, and human evil on a collective scale? What is the process for restoring justice when the victimizer/violator is the state and the victims are teachers, church leaders, professors, students, union leaders, clergy, nuns, laypersons, leaders and members of indigenous groups, and a host of others? Or when the perpetrators include Christian brothers and sisters? How can the memory of what happened be recovered so that the truth about past violations of human rights can be confessed and publicly acknowledged? What does justice mean, and how can healing and wholeness be restored to the community? What is required so that repentance, forgiveness, and reconciliation may occur? How can people work together to transform their communities and their nations?

Around the globe, in a variety of contexts, a process of democratization is currently underway. Civil war, dictatorship, and totalitarianism are slowly being replaced by more participatory forms of government. In the midst of these transitions, religious leaders, victims, survivors, and human rights activists are asking serious questions about past as well as recent human rights violations. They are engaged in an effort to avoid false reconciliation, with the hope of achieving true restorative justice. They firmly believe that the first step toward restorative justice is taken when governments and civil society tell the truth about past atrocities carried out by the state. "It is a search for the truth which heals divisions through promoting sincere dialogue and truth-telling, which enables a context such that forgiveness may be possible, which promotes justice—all of which can lead to true rather than false reconciliation."[1] The challenge is not only to break the silence about past violations. It is also a call for perpetrators to admit their sin and ask for pardon, and to provide the evidence for appropriate prosecution within the judicial process.[2] It is a call for the creation of a space and a context in which survivors remember and tell the story so that their loved ones' ending can be completed; where the violators remember, confess, and offer repentance; a space where forgiveness is offered; a field where the seeds for reparation and reconstruction are sown. Without memory there is no healing, and without forgiveness there is no future, says Peter Storey, past president of the Methodist Church of South Africa and member of the selection committee for the South Africa Truth and Reconciliation Commission.[3] Memory, truth-telling, repenting, and forgiving, with hope for healing and wholeness.

Examining Truth Commissions

This thing called reconciliation . . . if I am understanding it correctly . . . if it means this perpetrator, this man who has killed Christopher Piet, if it means he becomes human again, this man, so that I, so that all of us, get our humanity back . . . then I agree, then I support it all.

—Cynthia Ngewu, mother of Christopher Piet, one of the Gugluletu Seven (South Africa)

During the past twenty-five years, there have been more than twenty truth commissions throughout the world. Perhaps the best-known and clearest examples of restorative justice on the national level are the Truth and Reconciliation Commission and the Amnesty hearings in South Africa. What is not so well-known is that the designers of South Africa's Truth and Reconciliation Commission first studied the truth commissions in Latin America that preceded it. These included Brazil's non-governmental truth-seeking project secretly prepared by the Archdiocese of São Paulo to document the systemic torture of political prisoners by Brazil's military regimes from 1964 to 1979;[4] Argentina's National Commission on the Disappeared in 1983-1984; Chile's National Commission on Truth and Reconciliation, 1990; and El Salvador's Commission on the Truth, 1991-1993. The South Africans learned that many of the truth commissions in Latin America had not been successful in getting the cooperation of the perpetrators of crimes.

Chile: The Rettig Commission

In September 1973, the democratically elected government of President Salvador Allende of Chile was overthrown by Chile's armed forces. With the assistance of the United States Central Intelligence Agency, and under the leadership of the Chilean army, commander-in-chief General Augusto

Pinochet, the military regime instituted a state of siege that ushered in seventeen years of military rule. During this period, the regime committed gross human rights violations. Thousands were kidnapped, imprisoned, tortured, murdered. Thousands disappeared. When military rule came to an end, a truth and reconciliation commission (known as the Rettig Commission), was established in order to facilitate reconciliation between the military and the hundreds of thousands of families who suffered during the dictatorship. The problem with the Rettig Commission was that it had no judicial powers. It could neither establish culpability nor impose penalties. Before handing over power, the Chilean military regime dictated a provision that impeded the Congress from investigating crimes of the dictatorship or from bringing constitutional accusations against its leaders for actions carried out during the military regime.[5]

One of the Rettig Commision's tasks was to document crimes carried out by the Pinochet regime—such as torture and exile—in the official history of the repression. Many of these crimes carried out by the state were not made public until years later.[6] There was no repentance by the perpetrators of the crimes because they did not feel remorse. In fact, nearly all of the dictatorship's criminals were motivated by ethics and convictions based on military values. They regarded their actions as completely justified because they had saved Chile from a subversive threat, bringing peace and stability to the country. For this reason, political or moral punishment did not create the slightest discomfort.[7] Nevertheless, the Rettig report printed the names of those who had been killed and disappeared during the dictatorship.

Many in Chile believe this was extremely significant. That the final Rettig report named victims was important in terms of restoring the honor of those who were killed or disappeared, particularly since many Chileans still believed that such atrocities had never taken place in their country.[8]

South Africa: The Truth and Reconciliation Commission

The president believes—and many of us support him in this belief—that the truth concerning human rights violations in our country cannot be suppressed or simply forgotten. They ought to be investigated, recorded and made known. . . . There is a commitment to break from the past, to heal the wounds of the past, to forgive but not to forget and to build a future based on respect for human rights. This new reality in the human rights situation in South Africa places a great responsibility on all of us. Human rights is not a favour, or a gift handed down as a favour by a government or state to loyal citizens. It is the right of each and every citizen.

—Dullah Omar, Minister of Justice
Introduction to the Truth and
Reconciliation Commission

In December 1995, the Truth and Reconciliation Commission of South Africa began a long process designed to recover the full memory of what took place in South Africa from March 1, 1960, to May 10, 1994. Signed into law by President Nelson Mandela on July 19, 1995, the Truth and Reconciliation Commission (TRC) consisted of three committees: Human Rights

Violations, Reparations and Rehabilitation, and Amnesty. The TRC was made up of seventeen commissioners who had been nominated by non-governmental organizations, churches, and political parties; interviewed in public by a panel; and then selected by the president and his cabinet. The commissioners had the power to subpoena and were staffed with sixty investigators. During a period of 244 days, commissioners participated in more than fifty public hearings and took more than 20,000 statements from survivors of political violence and their families. The Amnesty committee received approximately 7,050 amnesty applications, 77 percent from prisoners. The final report of the Truth and Reconciliation Commission consists of five thick volumes that include reports about methodology, concepts, principles, legal challenges; an overview of the activities of the state and liberation movement during apartheid; human rights abuses in every province and regional political conflict; the role of businesses, churches, media, prisons, and compulsory military service; a list of the victims of human rights violations and the context in which the violations took place; and a reparations policy, findings, and recommendations for avoiding future abuses.

The Truth and Reconciliation Commission was covered by the media worldwide. From the outside, there was a sense among many that the TRC was going to resolve the problems of apartheid in South African society, clearing the way for the construction of a new nation-state. Yet within South Africa, many people—perpetrators and victims alike—were not happy with the TRC. Perpetrators wanted to minimize truth-telling, so that they and the nation could put the past behind them and move into the future. Amnesty was the critical element that ensured the participation of some Afrikaners. But amnesty was problematic for many of the victims and their families. As H. Russel Botman and Robin M. Peterson, senior lecturers at the University of the Western Cape pointed out at the time, "Victims want the dignity of their loved ones restored, their remains properly buried, and the nation to have an indelible memory of what has happened in this country in the name of a Christian government, but they remain ambivalent about the granting of amnesty to perpetrators."[9] Many South Africans believed the granting of amnesty to perpetrators meant that victims—ordinary citizens—would not be able to file a civil claim in court. Two weeks before the hearings began, many challenges emerged, including one on the question of amnesty. As Archbishop Desmond Tutu explained, amnesty was the political trade-off: "We did not decide on amnesty, the political parties decided on amnesty. Amnesty made our election possible. The amnesty clause was inserted in the early hours of the morning after an exhausted night of negotiating. The last thing, the last sentence, the last clause, was added: amnesty shall be granted through a process of reconciliation. And it was only when that was

put in, that the boere signed the negotiations, opening the door to our election."[10] Other criticisms of the TRC included the lack of direct victim-offender encounter during the life of the TRC; and the fact that not much restitution was carried out by the victimizers/offenders.

Did the Truth and Reconciliation Commission create a space, an opening, for South Africans —victims and perpetrators alike—to tell and hear the truth? Antjie Krog, an Afrikaner poet and journalist who covered the TRC, tells of an exchange between Nadine Gordimer, the white South African writer who won the Nobel Prize in Literature, and a black writer. "Why do you always picture a white woman lounging next to a swimming pool?" asked Gordimer. "We are not all like that!" He replied, "Because we perceive you like that." Says Krog, "Gordimer admits that she has to take cognizance of that truth." If restorative justice is meant to create comprehension of who was harmed and their needs; to determine whose obligation they are; to transform the system that allowed the injustice to take place; and to provide for public confession and acknowledgment so that there can be healing and wholeness for the community, then what role does truth play?

If the perpetrators will come forth with the truth if there is a guarantee that they will not have to "pay" for their actions, will that restore justice? If the perpetrators indeed tell the truth, but continue to believe that what they did was right and therefore do not repent, no matter how horrendous the atrocities committed, then what will restore justice to the community? If perpetrators don't care about receiving forgiveness or about reconciling with their victims, how will commu-

nities and nations be transformed? Dr. Farid Esack, a Muslim theologian and academic who testified before the commission gives one answer: "The only truths we were told were those the perpetrators feared were going to come out in any case. The agents of the apartheid regime confessed only to the barest minimum required to get them off the hook. As for reconciliation, those who needed to hear those truths most of all, the Whites of South Africa, were essentially absent throughout the proceedings." (Esak, Farid. *On Being a Muslim*. Oxford: One World Publications, 2000, p. 187.)

Krog, whose own Afrikaner family benefited from apartheid, provides another answer to the question of truth and the role of the TRC: "If its interest in truth is linked only to amnesty and compensation, then it will have chosen not truth, but justice. If it sees truth as the widest possible compilation of people's perceptions, stories, myths, and experiences, it will have chosen to restore memory and foster a new humanity and perhaps that is justice in its deepest sense."[11]

As the TRC traveled throughout South Africa to gather testimonies and receive petitions for amnesty, the apartheid divide was reflected in the TRC's audience. Most whites did not want to listen to the testimonies. One white woman told Krog, "I don't even watch the Truth Commission on television—because all you see is a sea of hatred." Krog responded, "I attend most of the hearings and that is not true. There is really no hatred."

This apartheid divide was graphically illustrated when the hearings moved to a town in the Northern Province of South Africa. Krog reported, "While the commission listens to testimony of human rights violations, cheerful white families with their Tupperware, sun hats, and small-town familiarity spend the day picnicking on the grass outside. Caught between the field and the hall, we in the media sit listening to bitter crying and choked words, interspersed with cheering and applause from an enthusiastic cricket crowd. The division carries through to the policemen patrolling the show grounds. The white policemen loll about, watching the cricket, while their black colleagues stand solemnly in the doorways of the hall listening to the testimony."[12]

Botman, president of the South Africa Alliance of Reformed Churches, and Petersen (cited earlier) lament that the churches have not played a more active role in the truth and reconciliation process: "Although there have been many things happening among the churches at a regional level, there has been little systematic reflection on the theological, moral and religious questions that the TRC process raises for the churches."[13]

Despite the failings of the TRC process, among the most powerful aspects of the truth-telling in South Africa—like Chile—was that the brutal reality of life and death under apartheid was unmasked for the world and the unbelieving white minority within South Africa to see. According to Alex Boraine, deputy chairperson of the TRC and director of the International Center for Transitional Justice in New York, "The truth that emerged in the stories told by victims and perpetrators challenged the myths, the lies, and the half-truths conveyed and distributed at every level of the former regime. I am unashamed in my belief that, in the South African context, history has to be rewritten and the TRC has made a significant contribution to this end. It is now no longer possible for so many people to claim that they did not know."[14]

Since South Africa's experience with the Truth and Reconciliation Commission, several African nations, including Sierra Leone, Nigeria, and Rwanda, are engaged in the process of implementing special courts and/or trials on a national level. In Sierra Leone, a special court is being established to handle trials arising out of the war in Sierra Leone under a treaty between the government of Sierra Leone and the United Nations. In Nigeria, the Human Rights Violation Investigation Commission, modeled after South Africa's Truth and Reconciliation Commission, opened public hearings in October 2000 to investigate human rights abuses from 1966 to 1999, during the military dictatorship.

In 2001, Rwanda reintroduced a nineteenth-century, pre-colonial legal system called *gacaca*, a form of village tribunal, to question those who in only 100 days carried out the brutal slaughter of 800,000 Tutsis and moderate Hutu. The tragic genocide in Rwanda is especially challenging for the churches. Nearly all of the deaths resulted from individual homicides carried out by an estimated half-million people. More than 100,000 people have been sitting in jails under deplorable conditions for more than five years. How will the community deal with the appalling reality that many of the killers were children? Rev. Ngoy Daniel Mulunda-Nyanga, a United Methodist elder who has provided important leadership in conflict resolution and restorative justice through the All Africa Conference of Churches and the United Methodist Church, says,

It is important to understand that the churches in Rwanda face a very troubling situation because they and the government are all survivors of the genocide. They share the same history and traumatizing experience. In Rwanda the situation is particularly devastating because almost every Rwandan lost at least one relative in the war, the exodus of the refugees, and the tragic genocide. To talk about reconciliation in the face of such suffering requires utmost faith in God. To embark on the ministry of peacemaking and conflict resolution is to respond to the call to carry the cross of Jesus and to follow him. To talk about the reconstruction of Africa is to offer symbols of hope. The churches are called to contradict the presumed reality of unending death, despair, and destruction in Africa with a reality of promises for a bright future.[15]

In the midst of these national tribunals, trials, and hearings, and at times in the shadows, religious communities and civil societies have quietly and persistently been carrying out a ministry of presence, peace-making, and restorative justice as they seek to bring healing and transformation to their communities. They are fully aware that hearings and tribunals at the national level are critical—if carried out with appropriate guidelines and criteria. There is also great need for models at the regional and local levels that can provide opportunities for people—victims and perpetrators—to ask serious questions about the past in an effort to avoid false reconciliation and in the hope of achieving true restorative justice. The experience of Guatemalan churches in the path toward peace and justice is an important example.

Guatemala: Recovery of Historic Memory

We found a woman. I called a soldier and I told him, "Take charge of this woman. She's a gift from the sublieutenant."

"I understand, my corporal," he told me and he called the boys and said, "There's meat here, you guys." Then they came and grabbed the girl. They took her little boy away from her and all of them raped her. It was a huge gang rape. Later I told them to kill the woman before killing her son so she wouldn't feel so bad about the death of her son.

—Testimony of a perpetrator in Guatemala, 1982, from the REMHI (Recovery of Historic Memory) Report

Guatemala's brutal history of violence, repression, and genocide dates back to 1524, when Spanish troops invaded the land of the Maya. From that period until the mid-1940s, little changed for the primarily indigenous people of Guatemala. Then, from 1944 until 1954, the nation experienced a brief period of democratization and reform: "For the first time, broad participation and civic organization influenced decision-making in public affairs. The growth of civil groups extended to labour unions and cultural organizations. Illiterate people (most of them indigenous) were recognized as citizens with the right to vote and run for public office, national industry and small and medium-sized agricultural production were promoted, a system of social security was adopted and important changes were made in labour and education policies."[16]

The land reform program, initiated by President Jose Arevalo to provide impoverished campesinos with farmland, resulted in the expropriation of large sections of unused United Fruit Company land. The expropriation was seen as a threat to United States interests. Following the democratic election of Arevalo's successor, Jacobo Arbenz, the United States condemned the social and economic reforms being carried out by the Arbenz government. In June 1954, the director of the Central Intelligence Agency, Allen Dulles, a former president of the United Fruit Company, organized an invasion of Guatemala carried out by Castillo Armas. The invasion and right-wing coup were successful. The United Fruit Company got back the land it controlled and changed its name to United Brands; authoritarian rule and repression returned, ending the brief period of democratization.

For more than four decades, Guatemalans lived a life of terror and death. Following the coup of 1954, they continued to organize political movements against repression despite the risks. After two brutal decades, Guatemalans believed the only way to overthrow the military regimes and bring democracy and freedom to their homeland was through a political and military struggle. In 1962, several groups joined to initiate an armed insurgency. These included the Rebel Armed Forces (FAR) and the Guatemalan Workers Party (PGT). In 1975, the Poor People's Guerrilla Army (EGP) and in 1979, the Organization of the People in Arms (ORPA) joined the struggle. In 1982, these groups founded the Guatemalan National Revolutionary Unity (URNG). In the same year, General Efrain Rios Montt, a member of the neo-Pentecostal Church of the Word, took power. General Montt employed an extremely brutal counter-insurgency campaign with the aim of turning the people against themselves. As many as one million boys and men, primarily indigenous, were forced into military service. Those who refused were tortured and often killed. During the first year after Rios Montt assumed power, more than 15,000 people were killed; thousands of popular leaders were "disappeared"; hundreds of villages and their inhabitants were annihilated; 500,000 were internally displaced; and 70,000 fled seeking refuge in neighboring countries. The testimony of one survivor from San Cristobal Verapaz, Alta Verapaz in 1982, gives witness to the severe brutality of Rios Montt's campaign: "The soldiers tied up every one inside the house without asking any questions. They poured gasoline on the house and set it on fire. Everyone inside died in the fire including a two-year old child. My mother, sister and brother-in-law died along with their three children."[17]

Finally in the early and mid-1980s, the world began to take note of the genocide in Guatemala—in large part because of concern raised by churches and non-governmental organizations. International pressure and the fact that the armed insurgency was no longer a threat, brought the Guatemalan government to the negotiating table. This happened despite a boycott by the URNG (Guatemalan National Revolutionary Unity), after the drafting of a new constitution and the election of a civilian president, Vinicio Cerezo Arevalo. The international community continued to pressure the Guatemalan government/military and the URNG to participate in negotiations. In 1987, the URGN and the Guatemalan government/military agreed to direct negotiations. Tragically, the years from 1987 to 1997 were defined more by armed conflict, torture, illegal detention, extra-judicial executions, impunity, and corruption than by the negotiations, which started and stalled throughout this period. At last, on December 29, 1996, the final peace accords were signed. General Board of Global Ministries missionary Paul Jeffrey writes, "The most significant accords worth noting were agreements dealing with human rights, the resettlement of refugees, the establishment of a commission for the clarification of human rights violations and violent acts that have caused suffering to the Guatemalan population, also known as the 'truth commission,' the identity and rights of indigenous peoples, socio-economic aspects and the agrarian situation, and the role of the army in a democratic society."

The churches in Guatemala, while supportive of the peace accords, were also frustrated. They were afraid that the accords would not be fully implemented. In 1995, the Catholic bishops of Guatemala, under the leadership of Bishop Juan Gerardi, organized the Recovery of Historic Memory Interdiocesan Project to assist the work of the truth commission. With the creation of a space in which people could tell their stories of suffering and pain, the project soon took on a life and purpose of its own. In the words of Bishop Gerardi:

> We were interested in discovering the truth in order to share it. We were interested in reconstructing the history of pain and death, seeing the reasons for it, understanding the why and the how. We wanted to show the human drama and to share with others the sorrow and the anguish of the thousands dead, disap-

peared, and tortured. We wanted to look at the roots of injustice and the absence of values. . . . Truth is the primary word, the serious and mature action that makes it possible for us to break this cycle of death and violence and to open ourselves to a future of hope and light for all.[18]

The process of developing the Recovery of Historic Memory Report (REMHI) was at least as important as its final outcome. Guatemalans participated in and directed the project. More than six hundred parish workers were trained to become interviewers, learning not only the technical skills of conducting an interview, but also how to address the social and psychological aspects of working with victims of violence and war. Many of the trainees themselves had been victims of violence.

They went through a systematic process of discussing the need to talk about what happened in the past; the reasons for preserving history; the value of giving and hearing testimony; and the mental health implications of reviving painful memories.[19] More than 6,000 interviews in more than fifteen indigenous languages and Spanish were conducted in those areas that had suffered the most repression. More than 200 Christian parishes assisted with the process. Perpetrators gave testimonies as well as victims. One parish worker reported that in all of the interviews he conducted with perpetrators, the men had to cry before they could talk. In four cases the wives of the men accompanied them, begging them to confess their stories so there could be healing in their families. As individuals and as community groups, victims told their stories. The REMHI project not only collected interviews, it also analyzed and organized them. A key element was the fourth and final stage when the results of the report were given back to the communities. During the fourth stage, the church offered mental health programs to the war's victims—a critical element of the project. Many mental health workers and victims have been forced to face the cruel reality that, despite the peace process and democratic transition, the people of Guatemala have not experienced restorative justice.

Mental health worker Rosa Lopez, a psychologist for the mental health team of the Archdiocesan Human Rights Office in Guatemala who worked extensively with the REMHI Project, says that she learned so much from suffering Guatemalans during the many years of marginalization, poverty, discrimination, and death. About the possibility for reconciliation in an unjust world, she offers the following comments:

> We don't think reconciliation is possible without a pardon, without acknowledgment of guilt or responsibility on the part of the state or the victimizers. We talk instead about putting closure on the pain. We try to ensure that the people themselves can find a way to heal their souls. We speak, for example, of returning dignity to the victims. Just recovering their bones, just carrying them in a coffin, just having a ceremony or a Mayan celebration is healing. So is the fact that the remains will rest in a cemetery where people can bring them flowers and candles, because the Mayan custom is that people go to speak to their deceased. They believe in a vital circle of life.

Recovering memory and truth-telling can be life-threatening. Perhaps Bishop Juan Gerardi had a premonition of the risk when he said, "The only ones who will help to build the reign of God are those who are able to confront the risks implied in the search for truth." On April 24, 1998, the Guatemalan bishop, head of the Catholic Church's Project for the Recuperation of Historical Memory (REMHI), made a public presentation of the project's final report, which included the following: direct victims of the war include approximately 150,000 dead; 50,000 disappeared; 1,000,000 refugees; 200,000 orphaned children; and 40,000 widowed women—a total of 1,440,000 victims. The report names the Guatemalan army as responsible for violence against 79.3 percent of the victims, and the guerrillas as responsible for violence against 9.3 percent of the victims. Two days after presenting the REMHI report, Bishop Gerardi was bludgeoned to death with a concrete block. It took more than two years to identify and convict the murderers. In June 2001, a three-judge panel convicted the following people of the brutal murder: Col. Disrael Lima Estrada; his son, Capt. Byron Lima Oliva; Jose Obdulio Villanueva, a former presidential guard; and a priest, Rev. Mario Orantes. During the trial, two of the three judges on the case and a prosecutor were forced to flee Guatemala after receiving death threats. On July 31, 2001, the lead prosecutor in the case fled Guatemala because he feared for his safety.

Bishop Juan Gerardi's murder has served to strengthen the church in Guatemala. In the words of Father Napolean Ruiz Rodas, a colleague of the bishop: "The Guatemalan church has risen to a new level of credibility. A church, a little more martyred and a little holier, that is a more credible church. A persecuted church is a church that has taken the right path."

Restorative Justice and Conflicts Unresolved

What role can restorative justice play in long-standing political and religious conflicts still to be resolved? In the case of Palestine and Israel, the Oslo "peace process" has brought no peace. Poverty, human rights violations, oppression, and hopelessness continue in the occupied territories of the West Bank and the Gaza Strip. Terror and death to Palestinian and Israeli civilians in Israel and Palestine continue, seemingly without reprieve. And in Northern Ireland, violence and death continue to plague the Protestant and Catholic, nationalist and loyalist communities despite the signing of the Good Friday Agreement several years ago. How might justice be restored? How are religious communities and civil society sowing the seeds of restorative justice in these two contexts?

Palestine and Israel

In the early hours of Tuesday, August 28, 2001, the bells of the Church of the Nativity in Bethlehem began to ring, and verses from the Qur'an were chanted from a minaret. It was not a religious celebration. Israeli military tanks, army, and bulldozers supported by Apache helicopters and jet fighters were entering the towns of Bethlehem, Beit Jala, and Beit Sahour in the Palestinian occupied territories. After promises that the Israeli military would respect holy sites and places, the army seized the premises of the Evangelical Lutheran Church of the Reformation in Beit Jala. The army occupied the church building; the Evangelical Lutheran Home, which cares for fifty children; and an inter-religious center and guesthouse used to bring together people of the three Abrahamic faiths for reflection and action. From the church sanctuary and grounds, Israeli soldiers set up a military outpost from which to shoot at Palestinians in the town.

Denunciations came from within Palestine, as well as from international religious and grass-roots communities. By Thursday, after international pressure, including calls from the U.S. State Department, the Israeli military pulled its troops from the premises of the Lutheran church. Although the mainstream Western press reported that Israeli tanks and troops were responding to Palestinian gunfire, Dr. Nuha Khoury and Rev. Dr. Mitri Raheb of the International Center of Bethlehem and colleagues of General Board of Global Ministries missionary, Rev. Sandra Olewine, told another story:

> Sarkis, an eleven-year-old sixth grader, has lived through an experience that no child should have to live through. On the evening of last Wednesday, when the shooting restarted, a bullet entered the main door of Sarkis's house, terrifying him and his family. To calm the children down, his mother told him and his sisters not to be afraid and to pray for the safety of the family. Before he had time to kneel down to start praying, two successive missiles hit the home, leaving him and his sisters screaming and crying. The missiles hit the chimney and the main entrance and left no glass window or door intact. Thank God Sarkis and his family were not hurt, yet the family is traumatized by the experience.

Angelina, a thirteen-year-old student, who is at the top of her eighth grade, has another horrific story to tell. Her home, which is in the area that was reoccupied, was taken over by the Israeli army and was used by the soldiers as a shooting base. Angelina and the other members of her family, all 13 of them, were locked into one room in the house for two days and were not allowed to get food or even to go to the bathroom without the soldiers' permission. Angelina and her family are physically fine, but the memory and trauma of being taken hostage in their own house will take a long time to get over. The stories of both Sarkis and Angelina are not unique. Please keep them and all the children of Palestine in your prayers.[20]

When the Declaration of Principles (DOP) was signed by Israel and the Palestine Liberation Organization in September 1993, many in the international community celebrated. The purpose of the DOP was to provide a process through which negotiations about the permanent status of the Palestinian occupied territories would lead to the implementation of United Nations Security Council Resolutions 242 and 338. Resolution 242 was adopted in the aftermath of the June 1967 Six-Day War and calls for Israel's withdrawal from territories it conquered in the war, including Egypt, Syria, and Jordan, in return for Arab acceptance of Israel's right to live within secure and recognized borders free from threats or acts of force. Resolution 338 includes the cease-fire which ended the war in October 1973, and added a requirement that negotiations include all parties concerned, thereby ensuring a role for Palestinians. The Declaration of Principles on

Palestinian women of different faiths

Interim Self-Government Arrangements outlined a process that was to last no more than five years and was to include "permanent status negotiations" beginning no later than 1996. The DOP and subsequent agreements, known as the Oslo Accords, were to resolve remaining issues between the Israelis and the Palestinians, including Jerusalem, refugees, Israeli settlements in occupied territories, security arrangements, borders, water, and relations and cooperation among neighbors.

Now, eight years since Israeli prime minister Yitzhak Rabin and Palestinian Liberation Organization chairman Yasser Arafat shook hands on the White House lawn, agreeing to postpone negotiations about the most difficult issues, the so-called peace process is dust in the wind. One year after the Aqsa Intifada began, life in the Palestinian occupied territories is much like a war zone. By the fall of 2001, more than 662 Palestinians and 160 Israelis had been killed and more than 15,000 Palestinians and Israelis (primarily Palestinians) had been wounded.

The 2 million Palestinian inhabitants of the West Bank and the 1.3 million in the Gaza Strip live under military closure. They cannot travel from place to place and must endure long lines at more than eighty checkpoints. Even though it is illegal, many students walk for miles around road blocks to get to schools and universities. Villages are subject to curfews, allowing inhabitants only a few hours every several days to look for food and other basic necessities. Numerous villages have been totally sealed off. For example, the closures of two villages near Nablus—Beit Fariq and Beit Dajan—lasted fourteen days in August and September, 2001. During this period, no residents were allowed in or out of the villages and transportation of food, water, and gas was forbidden.

Water is controlled by the Israelis. Palestinian property continues to be seized and destroyed: 150,000 olive and citrus trees have been uprooted; 2000 homes demolished; acres of land destroyed or expropriated for Israeli military settlement. Palestinian farmers or business people cannot export to any Arab country directly, but must send their products through Israel. The unemployment rate in the Palestinian population is higher than 60 percent and the rate of poverty is 50 percent. At the same time, some 400,000 Israeli Jewish settlers living in the 140 settlements throughout the West Bank and Gaza travel on their own roads to work in Israel; may legally carry and use weapons; have unlimited use of water; have modern schools, health care facilities and recreational areas for their own use; and are not subject to checkpoints, closures, or any other rules of military occupation. The Israeli government continues its policy of extra-judicial executions of Palestinian leaders and the bombing of police stations, schools, and homes. While the Israeli mili-

tary uses the latest in U.S.-built and supplied F-16s, helicopter gun ships, tanks, and missiles, combined with its Navy and intelligence apparatus, the Palestinians fight back with small weapons. They have no armor, artillery, air force, army, or navy.

In the midst of the violence and ongoing occupation, what can be done to address the critical need for restoring justice to Palestine and Israel? Zoughbi Zoughbi is a Palestinian Christian who founded the Wi'am Palestinian Conflict Resolution Center in Bethlehem, Palestine, in 1995. Wi'am helps to resolve disputes within the Palestinian community by combining the traditional Arab form of mediation called *sulha*, with Western models of conflict resolution. As Wi'am became more involved in resolving conflicts, it became clear that it needed to take a more aggressive role in their prevention. Along with direct mediation, Wi'am works with people in the community, focusing on youth and young adults, training them in the areas of human rights and democracy. Resolving and preventing conflicts has become a community effort involving families, youth, children, and local government, says Zoughbi. As a result of the massive increase in violence over the past year, Wi'am has responded to the tremendous crisis of children in trauma. Many children, like Sarkis and Angela, have lost their sense of security and show signs of psychological disorders, including nightmares, bed-wetting, tension and obsession. In response, Wi'am developed a trauma-healing project that is carried out in schools, families, and neighborhoods. Providing ministries of training, counseling, and guidance, and a safe haven when responding to situations of violence and conflict, is critical. Nevertheless, those who advocate restorative justice believe that more is needed in places where human rights violations continue and national or regional conflicts have not been resolved. The key in the context of Palestine and Israel is to end the Israeli occupation of Palestinian lands. In the meantime, those committed to restorative justice must work toward minimizing the gap between victim and oppressor, says Zoughbi. Concretely, this means supporting projects of capacity-building aimed at empowering the Palestinian community. Zoughbi says it also requires "that we develop different sources of power, moral power, narration of history, legitimacy, and unity of the conquered/oppressed peoples. It requires that we find a way to empower the Palestinians and help the Israelis to get rid of being the occupier."[21]

Northern Ireland

"You call it 'the war on terrorism'; we call it 'the troubles,'" reflected Rev. Gary Mason, Methodist pastor from Belfast, Northern Ireland, during a visit to the United States in early October 2001, only weeks after the tragedies of September 11.

The conflicts between the Protestant and Catholic communities living in the northern part of Ireland, distinct in their religious and cultural roots as well as histories, may be traced back for centuries. However, when people speak of "the troubles" they are speaking of the more violent period from 1968 to 1999 when nearly 4,000 people died in the conflict. Today, three years after the signing of the Good Friday Agreement—an election in which almost 72 percent of the voters in Northern Ireland and just over 96 percent of

the electorate in the Republic of Ireland approved the agreement, and movement toward integration to establish new forms of government ending British rule in the North and setting up of a North-South Council for joint representation—the troubles are still not over. "We have benign apartheid," explains Glenn Jordan, a former Catholic who works with Rev. Mason at the East Belfast Mission. "People live together (albeit in segregated communities), but there is still this hatred. Whenever the climate is right, 'killing is okay.'"

What is required, say Mason and Jordan, is meaningful engagement. People must get below the surface to deal with the pain, to talk about it. Getting below the surface requires dealing with the sectarianism within oneself. Many middle-class Protestants will say, "I'm not sectarian," says Jordan. "But if they don't have guns in their hands, they have guns in their hearts. It is an unspoken and respectable sectarianism."

"Dialogue is risky," says Mason. "The mistake the Irish church made was that we didn't begin early enough. We have done ministry pastorally and focused inwards. We didn't have the energy or the resources to look outward into the community, which was torn apart by violence and conflict. We weren't willing to ask the church community questions which they would not ask themselves." For Mason, the risk meant meeting with and getting to know Protestant paramilitaries living in his community. He was struck by the discussions in the U.S. press following the September 11 attacks about the profile of terrorists. In the Irish context, said Mason, "People who are terrorists are on my church books; they hug their children; they make love to their partners. They served time in prison.

Eighty percent of our prison population would not be there if it had not been for the troubles." Mason reflects on his two best friends, growing up, with whom he went to Sunday school and played soccer. As young men, all three were invited to join a Protestant paramilitary organization. One was shot in the back and died, the result of paramilitary violence. Another is serving a life sentence for slitting someone's throat in an act of paramilitary violence. The third, Gary, became a Methodist pastor. (Interview with Glenn Jordan and Gary Mason, October 2001)

Ironically, one of the places where Protestants and Catholics were able to "get below the surface" during the troubles was in prison. The story of Jim Wilson is a case in point.

The sign on the wall behind Jim's desk is small and the letters are difficult to read unless you are standing next to it, up close. "I object to violence because when it appears to do good, the good is only temporary and the evil it does is permanent." It is an unlikely wall hanging for a former loyalist political prisoner who went to prison as a teenager, serving a sixteen-year sentence for murder.

When he was growing up, Jim, a Protestant, lived a few yards from Rev. Ian Paisley's church. "He fired people up, myself included," says Jim. His identity was staunchly Orange loyalist. He and his friends were committed to protecting the British Crown and state. "We were so impressed with unionism and loyalism. At an early age we took up the Royalist cause and took up arms. We were sectarian and didn't know any better. We were afraid of the Catholics taking over," he remembers. As teenagers, Jim and his friends were asked to provide security for one of the Protestant paramilitary

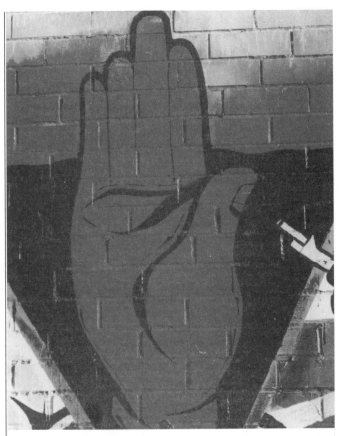

Wall painting in Belfast by a political group

organizations. Security included assassinations, bombings, and robberies. Jim was one of the vanguard of the loyalist cause when he was arrested and imprisoned as a youth.

It was during the long period in prison that Jim found time and space to reflect and meet others like himself, except that they were Catholic. "People say it was a religious war. It wasn't. It was a class war," he says. Protestants and Catholics who were fighting each other on the outside, began meeting and talking with each other on the inside. Outside the prison they reacted to what was happening in their communities. Inside, Jim found that he had more in common with Catholic youth and young adults from working-class communities who had struggled to get by in the depressed economic context than he did with the many staunchly loyalist leaders from Northern Ireland's upper-class Protestant community. It was this connection to "the other" that profoundly transformed Jim and many other paramilitaries like himself. When asked if he felt abandoned by the churches while he was in prison, Jim responded that Protestant ministers didn't visit the political prisoners much. "When ministers did come around they didn't want to talk about what really mattered. I think the priests on the Catholic side were more supportive."

Among the stumbling blocks to implementation of the Good Friday Agreement is the decommissioning of weapons so they are "permanently verifiably beyond use." On October 22, in an historic move, Sinn Fein[22] party leaders called upon the Irish Republican Army to begin dismantling its arsenal of weapons. Martin McGuinness, Sinn Fein deputy to President Gerry Adams and minister of education in Northern Ireland, reflected upon the impact of the recent terrorist attacks within the United States and on Sinn Fein's call to decommission. "For me, the events of September 11 in New York and Washington and Pennsylvania have given added urgency and incentive to those of us in Northern Ireland who want to bring our peace process to a conclusion,"[23] he said. Decommissioning continues to be a contentious issue in both communities because trust and respect is still lacking.

With ongoing attacks by paramilitaries who do not support the Good Friday Agreement, coupled with fear and an absence of trust between the two communities, many Protestants and Catholics do not favor decommissioning. "Unionism will not be left in a position where we

are vulnerable to offshoots of the IRA," said Jim in December 1999. "The paramilitaries in our circles won't use weapons as a first strike, only in the defense of our people. If we can get people to say, 'Weapons are not being used here,' we don't need decommissioning. In 1912, the Ulster Volunteer Force brought in 30,000 guns. We were never decommissioned. Guns being silent is enough for me. If I turn my gun in today, I can turn around and buy a weapon or commercial explosives tomorrow." But Bernie Laverty, a former Catholic who coordinates restorative justice projects with Protestant and Catholic women through Forthspring Community Center in Belfast is troubled by this hard line: "People say you can't decommission fertilizer, but isn't handing over weapons a symbolic act?" (From interviews in Belfast, December 1999)

Given this context, what kinds of actions and strategies will bring about restorative justice? Mason and Jordan believe that the road to restoring justice is built "one relationship at a time." What is required is to "hear each others' stories and pain."

In Northern Ireland, in the midst of "benign apartheid," creating a space for sharing stories and discussing issues is particularly challenging for people who have lived totally segregated lives within their Protestant or Catholic communities and have learned from an early age not to speak about politics or religion. Springfield Road Methodist Church, which sits along the "peace line" in Belfast, has created a space, called Forthspring Community Center, for Protestants and Catholics to meet together. Norinne Christian, a Dominican nun and founding member of the interfaith Currach Community, has worked for years to carry out cross-community work, bringing together small groups of Protestants and Catholics to learn about each other and develop mutual trust. Norinne worked with women from Springfield Road Methodist Church and others in the community to organize an ecumenical women's group at Forthspring. "Our people never discussed politics or religion, even within their own community. We realized we needed to teach people how to talk about politics," she said. Protestant and Catholic women from the area neighborhoods began to come together very slowly. It took two years of weekly meetings before they would look at anything together. After the women learned to know each other, they discovered that they had a range of similar concerns: poverty, unemployment, housing, community development, public education, health care, reproductive rights, domestic violence, community relations, and human rights, among others. Says Norinne, "I see our work as continuing to build relationships, building trust, offering programs for people to come here and test out what it means to be with the other. It takes time."

Mairead Corrigan Maguire and Betty Williams, winners of the Nobel Peace Prize for their leadership in founding the Peace People movement in Northern Ireland in 1976, also understand the critical role of community-building as part of restorative justice. Maguire writes, "The only solution to deep ethnic conflict, the only way to reduce fear, is to increase tangible human contact by bringing divided people together. . . . Human beings need to love and be loved, to feel a sense of dignity, acceptance, and respect, and this can be received only

through human contact." Maguire also speaks of the challenge in addressing the apartheid that is endemic in Northern Ireland. "Belfast, for example, has fourteen walls that, sadly, keep our people segregated. Our schools are segregated too. This division leads to further fear and mistrust. We have to do all we can to build trust. One of our Peace People programs offers transportation by bus for loyalist and republican wives and children so they can visit their relatives in prison. This bus takes people from one community to another community and allows individuals who often fear each other to sit, ride, and communicate with one another."[24]

Another crucial arena for community work in Northern Ireland is with young people and their communities—the focus of many former paramilitaries like Jim. For more than twenty-five years, paramilitaries have used a "graduated system of sanctions" to address crime and anti-social behavior within communities. Instead of turning to the police—who were absent in most working-class areas during the political conflict—the community asked paramilitaries to mete out punishment to perpetrators. The graduated system of punishment includes beating (such as breaking the knee caps), shooting, and exile. When someone's house is burglarized by a youth, that person will turn to Jim and other paramilitaries. "People are asking us to shoot the kids, or if we won't shoot 'em, to break their legs." Instead, Jim and other former political prisoners work with organizations like Alternatives, a restorative justice program established in the Greater Shankill area of Belfast. The program, in a Protestant working-class neighborhood, seeks to persuade people that a system which relies on violence is counterproductive; to eradicate punitive beatings; to heal relationships between the community and statutory agencies using a restorative justice approach; and to promote debate and discussion about the justice system and other methods. Alternatives has been successful in enabling youth to address causes of anti-social behavior and to set achievable goals for themselves. It has also been successful in preventing paramilitary punishment by providing the community with a visibly successful alternative. Of critical importance to the program's success is its commitment to clear principles of equality, dignity, peace, and democracy.

As in South Africa, restorative justice will not come to Northern Ireland because of a quick fix by politicians. It requires the slow, patient, steadfast commitment of people within the Protestant and Catholic communities. As Norinne Christian said toward the end of 1999, "For years we didn't trust the politicians and did the slow work on the ground. Like peeling away the skin of an onion. Now people are cautious. My fear is that people will assume that with the peace process no more work needs to be done. But now the work really begins, the work of changing people's attitudes."[25]

Springfield Road Methodist Church: located at the border between the divided Protestant/Catholic communities

Endnotes

1. Lucia Ann McSpadden, Foreword from *Recovering Memory: Guatemalan Churches and the Challenge of Peacemaking*, by Paul Jeffrey. Uppsala, Sweden: Life and Peace Institute, 1998, p. ii.

2. Ibid., p. iv.

3. Peter Storey, Presentation to Restorative Justice Ministries Inter-Agency Task Force, February 9, 1999.

4. See *Torture in Brazil: A Shocking Report on the Pervasive Use of Torture by Brazilian Military Governments 1964-1979.* New York: Vintage Books 1986.

5. Tomás Moulian, "A Time of Forgetting: The Myths of the Chilean Transition," *NACLA,* September/October 1998, p. 17.

6. For example, in August 2000, Rev. Enrique Vilches, a Methodist pastor in Chile, sent letters to the families of the disappeared informing them that a retired colonel of the Chilean armed forces had confessed to him that he had participated in dumping hundreds of political detainees into the sea in 1973.

7. Ibid., p. 19.

8. Ibid., p. 19.

9. H. Russel Botman and Robin Peterson, *To Remember and to Heal,* p. 10.

10. Antjie Krog, *Country of My Skull: Guilt, Sorrow, and the Limits of Forgiveness in the New South Africa.* New York: Three Rivers Press, 2000, p. 31.

11. Ibid., pp. 21, 22.

12. Ibid., p. 259.

13. H. Russel Botman and Peterson, *To Remember and to Heal,* p. 12.

14. David C. Anderson, "What Kind of Justice," *Ford Foundation Report,* Summer 2001, p. 29.

15. Mulunda-Nyanga, Ngoy Daniel, *The Reconstruction of Africa: Faith and Freedom for a Conflicted Continent.* Nairobi, Kenya: AACC, 1997, pp. 102 ff.

16. T. Palencia Prado, *Peace in the Making: Civil Groups in Guatemala.* London: Catholic Institute for International Relations, August 1996, p. 4 (as quoted in *Recovering Memory*).

17. Case 3164, REMHI report, p. 82, vol. 1.

18. Bishop Juan Gerardi, "Breaking Silence in Guatemala," Presentation of REMHI report in *Challenge: Faith and Action in the Americas,* vol. 9, no. 1, Spring 1999, pp. 10, 11.

19. The war was accompanied by a total psychological war—a war of terror that left open wounds and planted fear, uncertainty, loneliness, sadness, pain, and feelings of loss, mistrust, and abandonment. It resulted in a lack of belonging, the loss of social and cultural reference points, and the ability to say, "This land is mine." Many people have returned to live in borrowed lands. There is a lack of identity, of belonging to a place. Fear prevails—a fear that stays in people. There is a rage that cannot be resolved, a rage people carry inside that they cannot get out. (Interview with psychologist Rosa Lopez, *Faith in the Americas,* vol. 6, no. 2, Summer 1998, p. 9.)

20. E-mail from Rev. Dr. Mitri Raheb, International Center, Christmas Lutheran Church, Bethlehem.

21. Interview with Zoughbi Zoughbi, Bethlehem, Palestine.

22. Sinn Fein (We Ourselves) is a republican political party organized throughout Ireland. The Sinn Fein party identifies itself as separate from the IRA, although some of the public still perceives the party as a political wing of the IRA.

23. "Sinn Fein, for the First Time, asks IRA to Begin Disarming," *The New York Times*, October 23, 2001, page A3.

24. Mairead Corrigan Maguire, *The Vision of Peace: Faith and Hope in Northern Ireland*, p. 54.

25. Ibid. p. 54.

Most incarcerated women have long been victims of abuse. Some of them are locked up because they killed or assaulted their abusers.

5

MOVING INTO THE CIRCLE OF RESTORATIVE JUSTICE

At this point you may ask, "How can I get involved in restorative justice?" The answers are several. In the first place, restorative justice is not a specific organization or program. Rather, it is a perspective, a set of values, an approach to doing justice. It is, in a sense, a way of life, a way of perceiving and acting on whatever comes our way; whatever we are living with, including our relationships with others in our family, neighborhood, workplace, and faith community.

If we find ourselves drawn to a restorative set of values, the next question may be, "How do I get involved in the criminal justice system so I can experiment and try to live out and apply the per-

spective that I am developing in my life and my thinking?" There are two ways: by choice and through circumstance. We can research, make calls, and eventually find a way to get involved in some sort of volunteer effort—or paid employment—that will give us the opportunity to explore what restorative justice means in specific situations. Or we can be dragged into the web of crime and justice against our will: as crime victim, criminal defendant, family member of victim or defendant, or as witness or juror.

"Web" and "quicksand" are metaphors that aptly describe the criminal justice system: a web—something that traps us in its sticky strands like the web of a spider; quicksand—a force that sucks one in more deeply the more one tries to escape. "Circle" is a more positive metaphor. It suggests that, no matter where or how one enters the system, one thing leads to another, then another, until the whole big picture takes on meaning and, sometimes, a life of its own. In an earlier chapter we met people to whom this has happened. My own entry was in 1972, when I began visiting a man in prison on a regular basis. Soon we were confronted with the Tennessee prison system's blatant racism against him, an African American. A week later he escaped—nonviolently—from his minimum security prison. Until this day he has not been heard from. And, almost thirty years later, I am still trying to change that system. In a sense, he escaped the web and I got drawn into it. Yet, in another sense,

Ekatarinburg Prison, where prisoners created a rainbow—God's great sign of peace

while he has to look over his shoulder for the spiders who want to entrap him once more, I am on the edge of the circle—with a good view of what's inside, but enough on the edge to critique it freely, intervene in various ways, and build bridges.

Later we will look at ways of becoming engaged in restorative justice ministries within the arena of crime and the justice system. But first we need to put on our restorative justice lenses and learn to see the world through them. To give us some practice, we will look at some common, concrete circumstances—for ourselves as individuals, for our congregations, for our communities.

Individuals

Examine the following hypothetical scenarios. Each one could happen to us or someone we know.

1. Jury Duty. You open your mail and find a notice from criminal court informing you that you have been chosen for jury duty. You are to report to the county courthouse in exactly two weeks. So you rearrange your schedule and prepare to put your life on hold. Sure, it's a hassle; but you believe in doing your civic duty, and, besides, it might be interesting to see firsthand how the mysterious criminal justice system really works.

On the day you report, you realize that you are being considered for a jury that will try a man accused of first-degree murder. The courtroom is full: it is a high profile case. The prosecuting attorney asks you questions about your experience with crime, your feelings about police and criminal suspects, your religious and moral views on capital punishment. You realize that the defense attorney and the judge will ask you similar questions.

As you look at the defendant, seated beside his lawyer, you feel unsure of yourself. You are filled with a mixture of dread and excitement. You notice some people in the front row, behind the prosecutor's table, attending closely to the proceedings. They must be the murder victim's family. You become intensely aware of the very high stakes. You think of Scripture: "I have set before you life and death, blessings and curses. Choose life so that you and your descendants may live" (Deuteronomy 30:19).

You are being drawn into what may be one of the most intense experiences a person can have: wrestling with questions of the life and death of real human beings—both the murder victim and the defendant. You are also face-to-face with one of the most controversial issues of our time: capital punishment. Finally, in your sudden confrontation with the death penalty, you are presented with many of the central themes of Christian faith: the creation of human beings in the image of God; the depth and power of sin; the need for repentance; the meaning of God's judgment and God's grace; the nature and work of Jesus as teacher, model, redeemer, lord; the responsibilities of a Christian disciple and a citizen; the relationship between church and state.

More Bible passages scroll out in your head: "Whoever sheds the blood of a human, by a human shall that person's blood be shed; for in his own image God made humankind" (Genesis 9:6); "Let anyone among you who is without sin be the first to throw a stone at her" (John 8:7b). So, think about where you stand on the issue of capital punishment: as law-abiding citizen, voter, taxpayer; as

one who has perhaps been a crime victim; as a possible juror in this trial; as a United Methodist; as a follower of Jesus Christ; as one who claims to believe in restorative justice.

How do you perceive the reality of capital punishment? Do you have a definite opinion about the death penalty? Perhaps you want to do everything you can to be on this jury in order to carry out your strong beliefs—either to persuade the jury to give the death penalty, or to do everything in your power to stop it.

2. Your Child Is Arrested. Your juvenile son or daughter is arrested for shoplifting or vandalism. How do you handle it with your child? your spouse? the juvenile justice system?

There are many questions. Did he/she do it? What about the victim? If you think or know your child is responsible, do you encourage him/her to take personal responsibility, go to the victim, tell the truth, offer restitution, and hope the victim will ask the prosecutor to dismiss the charges or see that the case is processed within a restorative justice context? If your child gives up her/his constitutional "presumption of innocence," and the victim is vindictive, your child has perhaps thrown away the best defense, in the view of the defense lawyer. If you believe your child is not responsible for the crime, how hard do you encourage fighting for his/her rights—as opposed to making a deal (plea bargain) in the hope of avoiding a more serious sentence?

If you or the other parent knows someone with clout in the prosecutor's office, the police department, or even the judge, should you ask for help to sort of "make it go away"? What about all those young people whose parents don't know someone with influence? And what kind of message are you sending to your child as well as to the victim? Or perhaps you don't have clout and can't afford a decent lawyer. Then what?

Perhaps you are inclined to let the system play itself out, letting the chips fall where they may, and hope your child learns something by being held accountable in the sense of being punished by the retributive system. What if that means jail time? Do you know the risks? Does your child? What could be the role of restorative justice?

3. *Your Child and Drugs.* Your son was picked up for possession of marijuana with intent to resell. He's been using a little and selling a little to his friends, but that's all, so there's no particular victim. You suspected it, but never confronted him. You are a moderate wine drinker and/or cigarette smoker, or perhaps "slightly addicted" to diet pills—all perfectly legal in your case, of course. What do you do? How does your son feel about the consequences of his drug use compared with the consequences of yours? How do you feel? What is the restorative thing to do? (Don't forget to look at related questions in Scenario 2.)

4. *Should You Keep a Gun in Your Home?* There have been several break-ins in your neighborhood this year. You've just been told of someone's rape in her backyard by a stranger. You and your spouse have never had a gun, but some of your friends and neighbors do, and others are getting them now. Some relevant questions: How often are guns in the home actually used to kill a guilty intruder? How often do they kill innocent family members or friends? Could you shoot to kill someone who broke into your house to steal rather than harm anyone? How would you know?

What if they were just leaving your property? Could you bring yourself to shoot them? Should you? Can you think of other options for dealing with the situation? What other means of crime prevention do you have? Should you move somewhere else, letting the threat of criminals drive you from your home and community? Do you talk with your neighbors and/or the police about organizing a neighborhood watch? Or what about starting a movement in your neighborhood to seek better police protection? What are your restorative justice options?

5. *You and Domestic Violence.* For years your husband has been yelling and cursing, occasionally even shaking you, but last month he hit you for the first time. Somehow you managed to get to the phone and dial 911, but by the time the police arrived, he had calmed down. You told the police there had been a misunderstanding, and, since there were no visible wounds, they left. Since then, your husband's manner can best be described as a patina of overly solicitous sweetness with a subtle but unmistakable undercurrent of threat and intimidation. Meanwhile, you cannot stand the sight of him. Part of you thinks that it's over, that you should leave him and take the kids. Part of you feels you have not been the best wife, but there is still love between you; that you should stay, try being a better partner, and hope he changes for the better, too. Yet another part of you is terrified of what he might do if you left, and besides, you have no way of supporting yourself and the children without him. You decide to look into mediation, in the hope that the two of you will be able to work it out. Is this the restorative thing to do? What is a hopeful and realistic solution?

6. Your Daughter Faces a Long Prison Term. Your daughter is in prison on a drug charge and will be there for a long time. But she was living in another state when it happened and not many people in your town know about it. Still, your neighbors and some people at church are beginning to wonder why your small grandson is living with you. You made up something the first time you were asked, and have tried to avoid the question since. You visit your daughter when you have the time and money to do so. You haven't taken your grandson along, but are wondering if you should. His mother wants to see him, but you feel a strong need to protect him from her and her situation.

She is such an embarrassment! And she makes you feel so ashamed of her. You don't go to church much anymore because you can't face the questions and stares when you take your grandson to the nursery. You took a second, part-time job to help support him and pay for your occasional trips to the prison. Honestly, between the two jobs, childcare, and those long trips every few weeks, you don't have time or energy for anything else.

Deep down, you suspect it's all your fault. You must be a bad mother. You'll probably mess up your grandson, too. You're really the one who should be ashamed. And you are. No wonder your husband left you and your daughter twenty years ago. Thank God—or somebody—that he left before you had more kids! You're beginning to ask yourself, Do I have any reason to live? Do I have any right to live?

7. Your House Is Burgled. While you and your family were on vacation, someone broke into your house, stole a lot of electronic gear and jewelry, and got away. Everything was insured, but your grandmother's wedding band can never be replaced. She gave it to you on her death bed when you were just seventeen. The police found some of the stuff, and they found two young men, seventeen and nineteen years old, whom the pawnbroker identified and whose fingerprints were found inside the house. But you still can't sleep well at night.

Someone at church does volunteer work with a program called VORP (Victim-Offender

Peer Conflict and Mediation Program

The peer conflict mediation program at the McCurdy School in New Mexico, trains middle- and high-school students to resolve conflict with words rather than fists, knives, and guns, which are often the tools of choice in their northern part of the state. Students and staff may refer someone else for mediation, or someone may self-refer. This program is the longest ongoing school mediation program in New Mexico. Mediators were trained for the first time approximately thirteen years ago. The New Mexico Center for Dispute Resolution trains students and adults, and usually has twenty or so trained students.

McCurdy's board policy encourages mediation for resolving all campus conflicts. It is used for staff-staff, staff-administration, administration-administration, and student-staff conflicts as well as for student-student conflicts. Because of such mediation, there have been fewer fights on campus. It's an amazing program, and the students do an incredible job as mediators. For student-staff conflicts, there is one student mediator and one staff mediator. An annual McCurdy Peace Maker Award—a huge honor—is presented at the final chapel of each school year.

Reconciliation Program). They work with selected misdemeanor and juvenile cases referred by the courts. You like the idea. You know these kids both have drug problems. You and your husband talk it over, decide to check out the mediation option, and you call the prosecutor's office. They tell you it's out of the question since they don't mediate felony cases. Being the slightly uppity woman you are, you promptly contact the defense lawyer for the younger defendant, who is all for it once she gets over the shock. Even better, she talks with the other defendant's lawyer and he's supportive, as well. And both their clients are willing. But the district attorney's office still says no. What to do?

The prosecutor makes vague noises about contempt of court, should you persist in sticking your nose into his business. Also, he wants you and your husband to be witnesses for the prosecution. You can't see that either prison or probation will do these kids a lot of good. It may have just the opposite effect. And you feel you have a right to confront them, tell them about your grandmother's ring, and ask some questions. You want them to know what they have done to you and your family, and you don't want them to do it to anybody else. The VORP people are interested, but seem unsure about pushing the prosecutor since that's where their case referrals come from. You're not sure they'll go to bat for you even though you want to use their services.

8. A Moral Dilemma. You're a police officer. You know there are (at least) two kinds of police: those who join the force as a power trip, and those who still think of themselves as "peace officers." You think of yourself as the latter. You are well-educated, still young, and a good bet for a more powerful position. You want to help shape your department into one that values community policing, restorative justice, a more diverse personnel base, and an end to corruption in its ranks.

To your dismay, you learn there is strong reason to believe that your ex-partner—who once saved your life on the street—is a dirty cop, and racist, to boot. He, too, is on his way up the career ladder. You have a dilemma. Do you confront him and hope he will confess—or convince you that your information is wrong? Do you break the code and turn him in, thus endangering your own career (and perhaps safety) as one who stabbed her friend in the back to get ahead? Do you do nothing and hope it blows over? What is your obligation to the department? to the citizens of the city? to your old friend? to the past and future victims of his racial profiling and brutality? What does restorative justice mean in this context?

9. How to Respond to Personal Injustice. You are African American. A police swat team on a drug raid breaks into your house in the middle of the night with guns drawn. Eventually it becomes clear that they have the wrong house, and the team leader, a member of your church, is very apologetic. He had been given false information by higher-ups in the department. Meanwhile you, your spouse, and your children have been terrorized, and your house damaged. The next day your husband has a heart attack—his first. He lives, but with significant heart damage. The medical bills are exorbitant. He loses his job. You need to take a second job. The kids still can't sleep. The bank is threatening to foreclose on your house because you are behind on the payments. Meanwhile, you see the chief of the swat team every week at church. He continues to be apologetic and concerned about your family's welfare. What is the role of restorative justice in this situation?

You and your husband take the Bible and your church very seriously. What does Matthew 18:15-20 mean in this context? What about the scriptural commands not to take your brother in the Lord to court? But how much should you ask your children to suffer because of your religious ideas when a good lawsuit might bring a favorable result?

10. Should You Seek the Death Penalty? Your nineteen-year-old son's car is highjacked and he is killed by an ex-con cocaine addict. At least that is the official police account of what happened. The likely assailant is apprehended. You and your spouse are divided on whether or not to seek the death penalty. You are against it, partly because your son was; your husband is for it. For him, only an eye for an eye can bring justice and possible closure. It is all he can do to let the legal system do its work instead of "taking him out myself," as he puts it. For you there will never be any closure, and justice sounds like a meaningless abstraction.

Meanwhile the defense lawyer is trying to make it sound as though your son started a fight with the killer, and that the killing was in self-defense. Knowing your son you cannot imagine such a thing. Increasingly the whole judicial process feels like an elaborate game of torture. Your son's death has just about torn your heart out, and now this charade is tearing your marriage and your sanity to shreds. What to do? Whom to talk with? Your pastor? The district attorney? A shrink? At times you feel that if you

could just be left alone for a few hours to talk with the defendant it could all be cleared up. At least you would know what happened. But you know that's crazy. Where is restorative justice? For that matter, where is God?

11. In Jail on a Drug Charge. You wake up with a hangover and find yourself in jail. They've got you on a drug charge and a soliciting charge. You left your husband and children three years ago to pursue your cocaine habit, and turned to prostitution in order to feed it. You despise yourself, and get drunk on cheap wine when you can't score cocaine. Meanwhile, you hope that your clients from last night didn't give you AIDS—or you them. If you could just get some dope, you'd be almost glad to be in jail and out of circulation for awhile. But you'll probably be out soon, like it or not, because of the overcrowding. You just hope they give you back all your things, because there was a good bit of cash and no one can prove it came from criminal activity.

As you try to remove yourself psychologically from the noise and madness of your cell and all the other women there, and go to that small place still left inside yourself, you think about your past. You wonder how and where your life got off on the wrong track, and if you'll ever find your way back—or if you want to. Suddenly, for the first time in years, you feel your big brother's hand around your neck as he forces himself onto you in the woods behind the house. Just a moment— then the feeling is gone.

What does restorative justice mean here? Is there a program in your city that works to rehabilitate prostitutes who are drug addicts? Would you try it, if there were?

Churches

The following scenarios are about situations that might affect local churches. As a member—perhaps a leader—of the congregation, how would you respond to these crises? Are they opportunities to explore the meaning of restorative justice in the context of a community that sometimes calls itself the body of Christ?

1. Your Church Is Vandalized. One night a mentally ill, alcoholic, homeless Vietnam war veteran breaks into the church, eats some food in the kitchen, sleeps in the lounge, and generally makes a mess of the place. The custodian finds him early the next morning. Or, let's say that a couple of neighborhood teenagers break in late at night (a neighbor sees them), do pretty much the same thing, steal a television set, and leave.

What does the church do? Let it go? Call the police? Press charges? Seek to have the case referred by the court for formal mediation from the local victim-offender mediation center after contacting the police and pressing charges? Seek informal mediation in the community or within the congregation, "handling it themselves"? What must the church "render unto Caesar" and what must it "render unto God"? Do the answers to these questions differ depending on the scenarios? Why or why not?

Does the church have any evangelical responsibility to the homeless man? To the boys? To their parents? What if one or more of these persons were or ever had been a member of the congregation, or had attended worship services? Would they have felt at home? Would anyone remember them?

What if the crime were altogether different?

For example, what if it were embezzlement by the church secretary, who was also the church treasurer? And what if it had been going on for many years, in small amounts that eventually added up to tens of thousands of dollars? Would it matter if she was, when caught, making $5.50 an hour, with no benefits except an annual week of paid vacation, after twenty-eight years of employment with the church? Does this church believe in restorative justice? What evidence is there that it does? When is this congregation going to commit itself to restorative justice? What would it mean in these situations?

2. A Mosque Is Fire-Bombed. The mosque down the street from the church house is fire-bombed and extensively damaged, presumably in retaliation for terrorist acts committed against Americans by others suspected of being Middle Eastern Muslim fundamentalists. Your pastor and the mosque's imam have a cordial working relationship, having appeared on interfaith panels and at community vigils after a recent terrorist attack on American soil. The imam approaches the pastor two days after the firebombing to ask if his congregants might use the church's fellowship hall as a place for prayers at certain times of day until the mosque is repaired. The mosque is prepared to pay a fee, with details to be worked out by leaders of the two congregations. The pastor brings up the imam's request at the next Council on Ministries meeting. You are a COM member.

What is your response? What is the council's response? What if there are families in either congregation who have lost loved ones in terrorist attacks? Would that affect the decision? Should it? Much consternation is expressed during the COM meeting about Muslims' alleged senseless hatred of Western culture, the Christian religion, American ideals, our way of life, etc. When a council member—a professor of Middle Eastern history—tries to speak of the historical and political context and background of the conflict, and the U.S. record of not always wise and moral intervention in the region, he is shouted down and ruled out of order. The meeting degenerates into shouting and name-calling. There is no official resolution. The next day, the pastor calls the imam and says he is unable to respond positively to the request.

What should happen next? What role could restorative justice play?

3. Prisons in Your Town. You live and go to church in a county-seat town that has sought to revive its declining economic fortunes by arranging for two prisons to be built in the county. There are several prison employees in the congregation: correctional officers, administrative staff, the prison chaplain. The county police chief and district attorney are also members. The congregation's youth group starts an outreach project that brings low-income youth into the group. With the encouragement of the pastor, some of their siblings and mothers start attending Sunday school and worship services. Gradually it becomes known that several of the families have moved to the town to be near their husbands and fathers who are serving time.

Tension builds, and eventually outright conflict breaks out between some church members, including the police chief, several of the prison employees and their families, and the pastor. The issue is whether the convicts' families should be welcomed by the congregation. The problem is complicated by the fact that some of the unhappy prison administrators and the police chief have become major funders of the church's budget. The pastor, the youth leader, and you—as president of your local United Methodist Women—begin to see your shared dream of a serious congregational ministry of restorative justice trickle down the drain.

What's to be done? Can the local struggling mediation center be of help? What about the district superintendent? Or the bishop? Can other members of the congregation, the United Methodist Women, and the youth group be organized to stand tall and strong? What do the dissident pillars of the church need? What do the prison families need? What could be the role of restorative justice?

4. A Survivor of Childhood Sexual Abuse. A woman in your church's United Methodist Women has told you in confidence that she is a survivor of childhood sexual abuse by her father. She has never confronted him or taken the issue to the police. However, during recent therapy she was encouraged to do both. Now that she has faced these life-shaping events, she is having a much harder time with sermons about forgiveness, which she now sees as sweeping things under the rug. She has always associated forgiving with forgetting, and since she now remembers more clearly what happened to her, and finds the remembering both painful and somehow strengthening, she doesn't want to risk a return to forgetting and forgiving.

The woman's father, also a member of the church, rarely comes because of his advanced age and near-constant care of his invalid wife. The pastor visits them regularly. Several times he has invited the woman to go with him, but she always declines. He wonders why.

The woman asks you what she should do. Should she confront the pastor about her trouble with his sermons, and tell him why she can't take communion with her parents? (She blames her mother for ignoring the instances of incest.) Should she confront them? Should she bring charges? Should she tell the United Methodist Women group about her dilemma? The whole church? Should she leave the church, since she feels so much bitterness toward her parents? Should she tell her adolescent children—who are very fond of their grandparents? Since the Christian church seems to have such a sorry history of oppressing women, perhaps she should just throw over the whole Christian thing and be done with it.

Could a restorative justice perspective help in this situation? How and where would one begin?

5. Your Church and the Complexities of Choice. The Shalom Zone, of which your congregation is a part, discovers that it has a good shot at receiving a major government grant for an inner-city project to develop peer mediation, anger management, and conflict transformation skills within—and between—a couple of rival gangs in your church's neighborhood. It would be part of the federal government's new "faith-based initiative." As you and other members of the Shalom Zone's board weigh the pros and cons of seeking this grant, you hear a vague and nebulous suggestion from one of the board members. It seems the director of the local government office that decides which projects get funded has let it be

known that your group's chances of receiving the grant would improve with a certain condition: that the pastor of your church, an effective community activist, lay off her demands for a living-wage law to cover all city employees and workers for businesses with city contracts. Why does the director care? The mayor, who appointed the director, has promised the Chamber of Commerce that he will resist a living wage law with every fiber of his being.

What to do? The grant is desperately needed. So is the living wage law. Your pastor is ardently committed to both projects, as are most people in the congregation and most of the other organizations that are part of the Shalom Zone. You examine your own set of commitments. Your first priority has always been nonviolence, embodied for you in the restorative justice vision underlying the grant proposal for the gang project. The living-wage law is more of an economic issue, you think. But then someone points out that most of the affected city workers and many of the workers for businesses with city contracts are African Americans, descendants of slaves. And you start thinking about the issue of reparations for slavery. Someone suggests that this has something to do with restorative justice, too, doesn't it? The plot thickens.

6. Your Church and a Sex Offender. A formerly imprisoned child sex offender who has been released on parole wants to join your congregation. He had treatment in prison, and is undergoing further treatment since his release. He is forthright about his past and his problem. He says he knows there will be special conditions and arrangements, including a complete loss of confidentiality, that will be put into place.

An article in *Interpreter* magazine (July-August, 2001) suggests a mandatory covenant between a paroled sex offender and his church, which would include the appointment of at least two covenant partners from the congregation to shadow him at church family functions and escort him to the restroom. Such restroom visits should be limited to emergencies, since as a general rule those facilities are to be off-limits. The article also recommends that he "not accept any leadership or representational position within or on behalf of this church," and that he write letters of apology to his victims, their families, his family, and members and supporters of the church, specifically not including a request for forgiveness. These recommendations are based on the belief that there is "an extremely low likelihood that pedophiles can or will change," and that "the church's primary responsibility is to protect children and vulnerable adults," which, it is suggested, "should balance any uneasiness about the perceived harshness of the covenant."

Do you agree with such a covenant and the assumptions that undergird it? Are these provisions necessary? Are they restorative? Retributive? How can we balance the need to be restorative with the responsibility to protect the church family? Hard questions.

7. Your Church: Faced with a Murder. There is a vicious murder in the community, and the victim is the son of church members. The family is devastated. Its grief and bitterness go on and on, seemingly never to be assuaged, and are constantly exacerbated by the judicial system's interminable delay and inconclusiveness. Many church members, initially sympathetic, become impatient with the intensity of their grief and start distancing themselves from the couple. The pastor is not exempt, and has difficulty in dealing with the family in ways that are helpful to them and tolerable to himself.

One day they come to the pastor and the Council on Ministries requesting that the congregation be host of the monthly meetings of a local murder victims' family support group. They mention that some of the group are looking for a good church home, and hope this church might be that home. They also ask that the pastor, a trained pastoral counselor, be present at the meetings as a resource person.

What should be the response of the church to the first request? What of the pastor's response to the second request? What is the place of restorative justice in this situation?

8. Should This Pastor Be Fired? An inner city church is profoundly concerned about drug use and associated criminal violence in its neighborhood, as well as racial profiling by law enforcement officials. The pastor points out that another related scourge in the community is the rapidly increasing rate of HIV/AIDS, largely due to the use of dirty needles. The pastor proposes that the church offer leadership in the community by inviting other neighborhood churches to join them in a comprehensive response to the situation:

■ A public meeting with the police to protest the disproportionate and brutal enforcement of drug laws in the ghetto as compared with a hands-off police strategy in more upscale neighborhoods

- A lobbying campaign in the city council and state legislature for more drug treatment beds and more government funds for the drug treatment of indigent addicts

- A series of ecumenical study forums, open to the community, on drug policy, including issues of harm reduction, decriminalization, etc.

- A peace initiative to develop relationships with—and ease tensions between—local gangs as a way of decreasing their power and violence

- A needle-exchange ministry to decrease the spread of HIV/AIDS

The church likes the plan until someone points out that needle exchange is illegal in the jurisdiction. After extensive discussion, the pastor acknowledges its illegality, reminds his congregation that challenges to slavery and segregation used to be illegal, too, and that being illegal doesn't make something wrong. He discloses that for over a year he has been part of a covert, informal needle-exchange project near the church, but not in the church's name. Many in the congregation are outraged and frightened. Some demand that the pastor be replaced before the next annual conference and that he move out of the parsonage by the end of the week. Cooler heads prevail, but just barely. Can a perspective of restorative justice shed light on the situation in the community, the situation in the church, and the behavior of the pastor?

Communities

How can the crime and justice system pull individuals and congregations into its web, or circle, forcing it to respond? Some more scenarios:

1. Your Town a Private Prison Town? Your town has a high unemployment rate, a skimpy tax base, and a hankering for new industry. A private prison company makes a proposal to build, "on spec," a new prison just outside town to house minimum-security prisoners from wherever the corporation can find them, probably not from your state. They promise many new jobs, significant new tax money, and vastly increased profits for local merchants. It sounds like a deal too good to be true. It is.

Because you have recently participated in a study at your church of the prison industrial complex, and because you have a younger brother who is a prison guard and union member in another state, you know more than most folks about prisons, private prison companies, and prison towns. For instance:

- Private prison companies sometimes lie about the security level of their prisons in order to persuade a community to buy into their project. Then, when escapes and violence inside a prison get bad, it's too late for the community.

- Prisoners' families often move into a prison community to be near their incarcerated loved ones. They tend to be very poor, especially with one wage earner behind bars. This means higher costs in social services.

- Most of the high-level jobs in a private prison tend to go to outsiders associated with the company rather than to longtime community residents.

- Correctional officers have very stressful jobs, and studies of prison communities show increased levels of domestic violence, alcoholism, drug addiction, and divorce.

- Many private prisons built on spec now stand empty. There is no available work force, and they are unable to contract with a jurisdiction needing that sort of bed space, at that sort of security level, in that place, with that company. So much for lots of good new jobs.

- Being a prison town breeds a certain kind of culture, like many military-base towns. If you and others are not prepared for that reality, it can be a startling and unwelcome shift in the tone and flavor of your community.

So, what do you do? How do you educate, organize, and mobilize your neighbors to oppose such plans before it's too late? Can the church be of help? How can you get your fellow townspeople to see the problems inherent in this proposal? Can a restorative justice perspective help?

2. Your School and Fear of Violence. You live in a relatively safe community, but publicity surrounding a rash of school shootings in other states has kicked off a campaign to adopt zero-tolerance policies in your local school system, as well as metal detectors, armed guards, routine locker searches and pat-downs of students, a stringent dress code, and a return to the old policy of allowing corporal punishment. All this despite the fact that school killings have been declining for the past eight years; despite the reality that zero-tolerance policies often victimize students for unintentional and innocuous "violations," and give problem students just what they want—the freedom not to go to school; despite the fact that repressive and intrusive policies can violate the civil liberties of students; and despite the fact that paddling only sends the message that whoever has the big stick gets his/her way.

You and some of your friends have what you think are better ideas:

- more counselors and social workers in the schools

- good alternative schools

- anger-management and conflict-resolution classes for students and teachers

- peer-mediation training and a peer mediation program for students in the schools

How can you introduce such thinking without being perceived as naive idealists and/or troublemakers?

3. Black and White Churches: Addressing Racial Profiling. You live in a city—Cincinnati, Los Angeles, New York, somewhere else—where racial profiling and police brutality seem to go hand in hand. It has become the single biggest flashpoint and barrier between the racial groups in the city, and threatens to become worse in term of igniting mass violence and repression. Police investigations routinely excuse officers' egregious behavior. The black community is calling for a civilian review board to air and adjudicate citizen-police disputes over allegations of police brutality and racial profiling. Your white downtown church is in a yoked partnership with a black church located in a neighborhood with a high rate of police violence. What does your partnership amount to, really? Is there any joint action the two churches can take? What?

4. Your Church and "Not In My Backyard." You and your neighborhood church are located in a community that is in the early stages of gentrification. Forty years ago it was a middle-class white neighborhood. Between twenty-five and thirty-five years ago it became a working-class, mostly black community. Now it appears to be moving toward becoming a middle-class white community again, with some African American and Asian American middle-class folk. A local non-profit agency with a long and good track record in the community has a large old house that it wants to turn into a residential group home for juveniles who are adjudicated delinquent—for nonviolent crimes—and are not facing imprisonment. The non-profit group would run the center on contract with the state as a community-based alternative to incarceration, providing an urban-village type of therapeutic community with professional staffing, family counseling, community discipline, victim-offender mediation, victim restitution, and drug and alcohol treatment (outsource) when necessary. The agency wants two elected representatives of the neighborhood association to serve on its board to help with oversight of the house and its program. It also wants to establish a community-based committee to work with the agency and the juvenile court to develop a model program in restorative community service. This program would make placements mandated by court sentences or by mediated victim-offender contracts—meaningful work, closely related to the offense, leading to marketable skills for the time that the offender begins to look for a job.

A zoning change is necessary for the project to happen, and the predictable "not in my back-yard" resistance is developing. Amazingly, your congregation is roughly representative of the community's demographics as they have existed over the last four decades: older white folk from the old days, middle-aged and younger black folk from the last thirty years or so, and a sprinkling of recently arrived urban professionals of several races. The members' opinion is divided about the group home proposal. Because your church has an old, strong, respected place in the community, the agency and many of the more progressive and liberal neighbors are looking to your church for leadership. Should the church just let the political process take its course? Should it intervene? If the latter, what can and should it do? How does restorative justice apply? Only in the vision of the agency's leadership, or also in how the church might handle its own internal disagreements and what it might offer the neighborhood? As a church member, as well as one who knows a thing or two about restorative justice, juvenile delinquency, and effective intervention in the lives of troubled kids, what are you called to do in this situation?

Thus far in this chapter we have explored ways in which individuals, families, and congregations can be drawn, involuntarily, into that sticky, sometimes consuming web of the world of crime and what we call the justice system. We have also drifted significantly into the more intentional sector in which individuals, congregations, and communities may wish to engage the criminal justice system and its many and complex problems and opportunities.

These have been exercises in learning to face hard and ambiguous issues—personal, ecclesial, and public—through experimenting with the thinking of restorative justice. In a sense we have been testing the ideas of restorative justice on tough, plausible realities, even as we learn a new way of seeing.

Now let us turn to a more proactive agenda.

For the remainder of this chapter we will be taking a journey into the circle of restorative justice, starting with some relatively simple and easy options for involvement. Gradually we will move on to what many find to be more difficult, complex ways of exercising Christian responsibility in this part of God's world. We will end with suggestions that require much of us in terms of sensitivity, courage, and skill. Think of this progression however you wish, according to your temperament: a steadily ascending climb, as on Jacob's ladder, into the more rarefied reaches of restorative justice; an increasingly challenging descent into the quicksand of violence and retribution—all for the sake of God's restorative vision.

Charity, Relationships, and Justice

United Methodist Christians and others can find many ways to be intentionally involved in criminal justice ministries, and all are important. But of these ministries only some—by their very nature—can contribute directly to the larger task of transforming the criminal justice system into one of restorative justice. A number of restorative justice proponents have found that there is a kind

of step-by-step logic of deepening involvement, each step building on the others. This logic can also take the form of a circle, so that one can step in at any point. There is no better and worse here. These ministries can all be good if they are done from a restorative—not a retributive—perspective. Generally we will be following a trajectory moving from charity to relationships to justice.

For many people, the first step is to donate money to a ministry or secular organization working to serve crime victims or prisoners, or seeking to resolve some criminal or juvenile justice issue. This can be important, especially if one moves beyond tokenism, for "where your purse is, there your heart is also." Or, in cruder terms, it is a test of commitment to put our money where our mouth is. For others, the first step may be prayer for crime victims, prisoners, and/or their families—in general terms or for particular situations. This can be an important entry point, because it is not possible to pray earnestly for people's well-being and at the same time hate them or be indifferent to their sufferings. Members of congregations might pray throughout Lent—individually and as a part of worship services—for murder victims' families, for death row prisoners and their families, and for all of us living in a violent society. It works best if we pray for individuals by name, and are provided with a brief biographical sketch, if possible. This may seem very little, but it is a way of struggling with the issues in a faith context without immediately being forced to take sides in addressing controversial issues such as, for example, capital punishment.

One might be a pen pal of someone in prison, writing to persons awaiting trial in the county jail,

Stories of People in Action

Helping Children Visit their Moms (or Dads)

Kevin, ten years old and living with his aunt, was ready for Mabel and Rudy Topping when they picked him up one hot summer day five years ago. Then they picked up his three-year-old sister, Karen, who lives with her grandmother. They began the trip from Charlotte, through the countryside of North Carolina, to Raleigh. They were going to visit their mother at the Prison MATCH (Mothers And Their Children) Center. But for Kevin, this trip was special.

"Mr. Rudy, I can't wait to get back to school!" exclaimed Kevin.

"You like to go to school?" asked the Toppings.

"I like to go to school, but I can't wait to tell my friends about my trip. I've been to see my mother before, but we never went this way. I can't wait to tell about seeing the horses and cows and bulls!"

Another time, the Toppings took Kevin and Karen to the Prison MATCH Center for a Christmas party with their mother. As Karen bounced out of the car and Mabel took her hand, Karen looked at her and asked, "Miss Mabel, why is momma locked up?"

Taken aback by the question, Mabel said, "I really don't know, but I do know she loves you very, very much and she'll be so happy to see you." With that, Karen pulled a school picture of herself out of her pocket, and said, "I'm giving her this today."

These are just two of the many memories the Toppings have of providing transportation for Kevin and Karen to visit their mom. Coordination for transportation of Kevin and Karen to see their mother was made by the Prison MATCH Center. Between visits, the Toppings send cards to Kevin and Karen, and, from time to time, they talk by phone with the children's caregivers.

---

or to inmates serving time in a state or federal prison, or to people on death row awaiting execution. Those uncomfortable about using their home address might use that of the church. Church groups can prepare care packages, or bags of toiletries or cosmetics, for prisoners—especially women—who cannot afford to buy such items.

Churches, youth groups, Sunday school classes, United Methodist Women, and United Methodist Men can engage in study series on crime and punishment, victimization, prison life, restorative justice, capital punishment, or other related topics. Bible study, videotapes, and guest speakers, as well as printed curriculum or other material, can enhance such a study. This will better educate lay folk, push them to struggle with the issues, and perhaps get them more personally involved.

Another level of involvement is to do volunteer work, on a regular basis, that will provide some kind of service to persons caught up in the criminal or juvenile justice system, whether as victim, prisoner, or prisoner's family member. It could be tutoring or mentoring with adult or juvenile prisoners or ex-prisoners, or with the children of prisoners. It could be hospitality and transportation for crime victims and/or prisoners' family members. It could be taking children to visit their parents in prison, or teaching parenting or life skills or decision-making classes for victims or prisoners. It could be babysitting for crime victims. It could be special camps for children of prisoners. There are many other options, such as those mentioned in earlier chapters. A suggestion: Try not to worry about whether you are working with criminal offenders or with crime victims. Both are in need of compassion and concrete assistance. If you want an experience in which these distinctions are radically challenged, do volunteer work in a women's prison or jail unit. Most incarcerated women have long been victims of abuse. Some of them are locked up because they killed or assaulted their abusers.

Such ministries of financial stewardship and generosity, correspondence, intercessory prayer, and hands-on direct service are truly significant and can become the seeds of even more profound work in restorative justice. Following are some examples of this deeper level of engagement:

1. As individuals, we can participate in already established one-on-one visitation programs. At state prisons, information about such programs is usually available through the chaplain's office. If you live near a federal prison, you can contact Prisoner Visitation and Support, a national organization that operates in federal prisons throughout the country. Or there are numerous programs in which church and community people go into prisons—either on a regular (weekly, monthly) or one-time basis—to meet with groups of prisoners for religious, self-help, and/or educational purposes. Some of the groups that operate such programs in many prisons are the following: Yokefellow Prison Ministries, Prison Fellowship, Seven Steps, Alcoholics Anonymous, Kairos, and Epiphany (for juveniles). Specifically United Methodist possibilities include Disciple Bible Study, Covenant Discipleship groups, and United Methodist Women units. For those who do not live near a state or federal prison, there is probably a nearby county jail or juvenile detention center with a prisoner visitation or group ministry program.

Individuals or church groups that cannot find an already existing individual or group jail or prison program, or cannot find the right one, might consider starting one themselves. This is often most successful when done on an ecumeni-cal, interfaith, or community-wide basis, so it is important to look for likely partners in the community and include them in the planning as early as possible. For all such programs, it will be necessary to develop and cultivate relationships with prison or jail officials, because they are the people who control access and must approve of your program if it is to have a chance of success. For federal and state prisons, and for jails in larger metropolitan areas, these officials are likely to include the chaplain, the volunteer coordinator, and/or the warden.

2. Another option is to focus on ex-offenders who are coming out of jails and prisons into the community. People who own their own business, or who hire for others' businesses, can make a huge contribution by agreeing to consider qualified ex-prisoners for employment. Others can do volunteer work for agencies serving ex-offenders, especially halfway houses. One network of ten or so halfway houses in several states—in which male and female ex-prisoners and college students live together in community—is Dismas, Inc.

Individual congregations might approach state or local corrections or parole departments and volunteer to sponsor and support one or more prisoners soon to be released or paroled (perhaps along with their families), in much the same way that many churches sponsor or "adopt" refugees from other countries who are new in a community. The New York Annual Conference has such a program, and they also exist in some other states.

3. Victims and survivors of serious crime are in great need of ministry. Here, too, there are numerous options. Individuals, churches, or groups with-

in churches can volunteer at battered women's shelters, rape and sexual abuse centers, government (prosecution or law enforcement) victim-services units, or community support groups for victims/survivors. Parents of Murdered Children and MADD (Mothers Against Drunk Driving) are the best-known national groups, but there are many local ones, as well. Individuals and churches can also look into the possibility of starting their own ministries with victims—offering individual support or crisis intervention, holding memorial and healing services, or offering other ministries.

4. Another option is to look for places where "criminals"—and "victims"—continue to live in the free community and on the streets, seeking ways to be involved in ministries with them rather than focusing upon those in institutions. One example is working with youth gangs to support individuals caught up in the gang culture, offering them alternative groups and mediating/peace-making ministries within and between gangs. This can be a risky business requiring much skill, but some inner-city and other congregations are engaged in this sort of work. Another example, of course, would be to become trained as a volunteer mediator or reparations board member, or a community sentencing circle participant, to do such work on a volunteer basis with a community, court, or church-based restorative justice center, victim-offender mediation center, or neighborhood justice center.

Many of the more deeply engaged ministries just described can lead to the development of an ongoing mutual relationship with individuals—victim, offender, family member, corrections staff person—whose lives are profoundly affected by the justice system. At this point in the journey, one may notice a subtle but decisive change. Suddenly things get really personal. Abstractions like "crime," "incarceration," and "the death penalty" become profoundly real and concrete when we talk about my friend the rape victim, the bereaved spouse or child, the prisoner, the condemned death-row resident, the convict's child, the public defender, or the correctional officer. When, as is usually the case, our friend is suffering because of intentional or unintentional flaws in the system or in those who run the system, we may feel led by the spirit to move beyond providing a service in a program, or doing a more-or-less controlled volunteer task. We may move into the role of personal advocate, speaking for one who has no voice. This signals a growing and deeper involvement on our part, and is the point at which—as some southern church folk say of their "radical" preachers— "We done left off preachin' and gone to meddlin.'" For this, we who have dared to go this far are likely to pay and are unlikely to be thanked, except perhaps by the one for whom we are advocating.

Especially if we have moved deeply into the criminal justice web, or the restorative justice circle, to the point at which we are involved in significant relationships and/or are taking significant risks, it is important not to be alone. We need to be part of a support-and-learning group of persons similarly engaged, in our church or our community, creating a new one if necessary. Partly this is for mutual support. Partly it is for mutual learning. Sometimes it is for collective action. It is highly probable that everyone involved in the justice system in any way at all, needs such a group.

Another example: It may be that in our efforts

to promote restorative justice through advocacy around issues affecting our friends ensnared in the criminal justice system, we encounter our own brothers and sisters in the church who stand in the way of restoration. There are many members of the United Methodist Church who hold jobs (governor, legislator, sheriff, police officer, judge, prosecutor, defense lawyer, parole or probation officer, warden, guard, prison chaplain, etc.) in which they make decisions that have a decisive impact on the criminal and juvenile justice systems and the lives of those caught up in those systems. Some of them are able to keep a creative tension in the relationship between their faith and their work, and find ways of working restoratively within a mostly retributive system. Others may seem to be fundamentally compromised—trapped in a web or system which continually demands that they do things contrary to the United Methodist Church witness and the gospel.

In such situations they probably deal with the contradictions like most of us, with a mixture of denial, cynicism, courageous struggle, and cowardly sellout. In such a context, the whole issue of accountability needs to be pushed, for example, with politicians and criminal justice officials who are members of the United Methodist Church but carry out the death penalty, which the church has opposed since 1956. But accountability can be taken more seriously when balanced by personal support. It is possible, for example, that the United Methodist Church's model of Covenant Discipleship—in which both support and accountability are honored and balanced with each other—may provide useful guidance in gently pushing our brothers and sisters to deal with faith and work issues in a context that is safe, but not without challenge.

It is very likely that in serious conversation with fellow Christians and others who are active in the crime and justice arena, we will begin to discover that there are patterns and similarities in our experiences and observations. For example, if several members of a local church visit individuals in the county jail, and if, during their sharing and storytelling, it surfaces that not just one or two, but four or five prisoners have trouble communicating with their lawyers, at this point a "problem" has become an "issue." If we have the necessary wisdom, courage, and commitment, we may now begin to work together as issue advocates—not just for our friends, but for all similarly situated persons. It is time for collective action directed at a perceived injustice. In this particular case, it is time to go together to see the public defender or the president of the county bar association. Another example: If crime victims and offenders with whom we work express a desire to meet with each other in a safe environment, but the defense lawyers and/or prosecutors block such meetings, we have work to do to make this adversarial system more open to cooperative and restorative options.

There are many ways of engagement in advocacy around systemic issues in the crime and justice web. One method is to work behind the scenes with tactically placed interventions like phone calls, private letters, and private meetings. (Here is where a personal relationship with a fellow church member in a "high place" can be very helpful.) But, sooner or later, one finds oneself engaged in the public arena, where issues are addressed through some version of political education and struggle.

Examples of ways in which individuals, church groups, and others find themselves involved in issue advocacy are community meetings, door-to-door campaigning around a specific matter, building coalitions for joint action, organizing or participating in outdoor vigils and other acts of public witness, conducting educational campaigns, testifying in public hearings of city councils and state legislative committees, running letters-to-the-editor campaigns, picketing, organizing boycotts, organizing lobbying days or networks, and—in some cases—engaging in acts of nonviolent civil disobedience that challenge unjust laws. Clearly, like personal relationships with vulnerable and suffering persons caught up in the nightmare of crime and/or what we call the justice system, such risky, controversial, public involvement in moral and political struggle represents a deep engagement in the web, or circle, of restorative justice.

Advocates are needed for many issues in the arena of the crime and justice system. Some of the most controversial are gun control, capital punishment, the war on drugs, police brutality and accountability, domestic violence, parole (especially of sex offenders), racial profiling, prison privatization, and hate crimes. It is important to note, however, that serious engagement by individuals, groups, or congregations in public advocacy around any of these issues will very likely lead to significant levels of stress, hostility, and conflict in one's own family, neighborhood, workplace, and church. It is best to be prepared.

Systemic changes in the direction of restorative justice for victims, offenders, and the community can be achieved through sustained issue advocacy. But the deepest, most transforming changes are realized when we cross yet another line in the move from advocacy for our friends, or issues that affect them, to becoming allies with our friends as

well—some of whom may formerly have been our enemies. In my own case, this has meant working with prisoners, prisoners' families, and correctional officers to thwart corporate-political efforts to privatize my state's entire prison system. For twenty-five years it has meant working with death-row prisoners and their families, murder victims' families, religious leaders, lawyers, and other citizens to stop my state from imitating those who have been convicted of killing others by killing them. Many in The United Methodist Church and elsewhere have spent all or part of their lives even more deeply engaged in the struggle to transform their communities of faith, their neighborhoods, and the criminal justice policies and practices in their states and the federal government.

Like many advocates for restorative justice, I have found that this alliance model of faithful community organizing and public witness represents a most profound and genuine solidarity and collaboration as we work together for greater fairness, justice, and reconciliation in the criminal justice system—for victims, offenders, criminal justice system staff, and the larger community. With the alliance model, "we" and "they" are working and somehow living side by side in mutual struggle, even though walls, bars, and razor wire may separate us physically. "We" are no longer in control. We have moved from ministry to or for others, to ministry with our friends. It is another way—risky, but rewarding—of engaging the powers and principalities in the spirit of Jesus. It also continues the movement from work through charity to work for justice, grounded in deep relationships and inspired by a biblical vision of justice which is motivated by love and incorporates love into itself: restorative justice.

*Why are so
many people
so miserable that they use
substances that endanger
their physical, emotional,
mental, and spiritual
well-being? If we could
answer that question we
would know what to do,
and it would involve something far different from "just
say no" and "lock 'em up
and throw away the key."*

6

RESTORATIVE OR RETRIBUTIVE JUSTICE: WHAT DIFFERENCE DOES IT MAKE?

The Incarceration Nation

In the spirit of Jesus' prophetic engagement with the dominant powers of his time, what changes are needed to restore justice to today's retributive criminal justice system? Perhaps the best way to see this is to contrast the restorative justice perspective with a number of powerful trends in the criminal justice system of the United States, an influential example worldwide. In this section we will weigh the human and material costs of the retributive attitudes and policies that are so powerful today.

The present boom in prisons should be brought to a screeching halt, with an immediate moratorium on prison construction. The savings should be used in ways more likely to reduce recidivism: 1) probation and parole programs to reduce workers' caseloads; 2) more staff to supervise and support those on probation and parole; 3) public education; 4) drug and alcohol treatment and education; 5) affordable housing; 6) early intervention with struggling families and at-risk children; 7) development of jobs that pay a living wage.

Poor and remote counties need to resist letting state and federal governments and private prison companies exploit their poverty with the myth that prison construction encourages economic development. In the long run, prisons are economic dead-ends, destroying community.

Dungeons for Dollars

The answer to the problem of downsizing government-run prisons is not to replace them with for-profit private prisons. Taxpayers will still need to foot the bills for imprisoning people, and they will have to pay for profits to corporate stockholders, as well. Furthermore, many legal questions crop up when the private sector takes over a previously public function. The government's efforts to avoid running our prisons limit neither its legal liability nor its moral accountability.

Experience with efforts at prison privatization makes clear that when public policy decisions concerning criminal justice and public safety are tied to profit and corporate political power, the public loses. Conflicts of interest, lack of accountability, and the government's abdication of its responsibilities mean risk to the safety and quality of life of all concerned: prison staff, prisoners and their families, taxpayers, and potential crime victims.

Victims' Rights

The current victims' rights movement is on balance a good thing, since it insists on fair and respectful treatment of crime victims by agents of the criminal justice system. However, it is in danger of being so revenge-oriented that it leaves little room for victim-offender engagement and the restitution and healing that can come from such encounters. Although crime victims have rights often not honored by our criminal justice system, public officials should not, morally speaking, carry out revenge in their behalf. Three groups previously discussed—Murder Victims' Families for Reconciliation, the Journey of Hope . . . from Violence to Healing, and Survivors Advocating for Effective Solutions—are examples of positive ways in which crime victims and their families can focus on prevention, restoration, and healing instead of retribution.

Policing Our Communities

Policies for policing that are consistent with restorative justice do exist. Police who do block-by-block policing walk the streets and develop relationships with people who live in the neighborhood. And with increased racial and ethnic diversity in the force, community police officers more accurately reflect the neighborhoods they serve. Civilian review boards that truly reflect the community and have sufficient power to adjudicate disputes between police and citizens are basically restorative. They can go a long way toward reducing police brutality and fostering better police-community relations. However, non-restorative law enforcement practices continue to be rampant, including the sort of zero-tolerance, stop-and-frisk, and racial profiling tactics that have led to the sardonic phrase, DWB (driving while black).

Juvenile Justice

The current ongoing erosion of the United States' distinctive juvenile justice system is fraught with peril. The trying of increasing numbers of children in an adversarial court system designed for adults, and the use of adult prisons to incarcerate those children, may have a serious unintended consequence: more young people who will become habitual and increasingly violent adult criminals, having been victimized by, and learned from, adult role models. Even more deplorable is the use, in many states, of the death penalty for juveniles. A juvenile court system with various mid-range sanctions—dependent on neither incarceration nor slap-on-the-wrist probation, and prohibiting the death penalty—would be more humane, restorative, and effective, as well as far less costly.

Mandatory Minimums

The use of mandatory minimum sentences for certain crimes, as well as rigid sentencing guidelines to reduce judicial discretion, together bear significant responsibility for the current rapid increase in incarceration, especially of low-level drug offenders. A combination of endemic racial and class discrimination in law enforcement policy and practice, coupled with laws with huge discrepancies in punishment for different kinds of drugs, account for much of the disproportionate confinement of minorities in both juvenile and adult prisons.

The U.S. "War on Drugs" actually amounts to a war on the poor. This is especially true for black and Latino/a young people, even though they are statistically no more likely than middle-class whites to use illegal drugs. Fortunately some advocacy groups, most notably Families Against Mandatory Minimums (FAMM), have made real headway in building a movement to roll back the use of mandatory minimums in the United States. The Women's Division of the General Board of Global Ministries, in addition to its advocacy for more drug treatment and education, has also supported the repeal of mandatory imprisonment for drug and other nonviolent crimes.

The U.S. Drug War

For decades, U.S. drug policy has focused almost entirely on cops, prisons, and military might. Little has been done with alternative approaches. A drastic shift in policy, emphasizing treatment, education, methadone maintenance, and needle exchange, would be far more effective in controlling drug abuse as well as the associated personal and property crime. Here the focus would be less on punishment and more on treatment, education, methadone maintenance, and needle exchange programs.

Society in general, and the church in particular, should be less obsessed with "stamping out drugs" and more focused on one simple question: Why are so many people in our society—of all ages, races, and classes—so miserable that they feel compelled to alter their reality, however temporarily, by using substances that endanger their physical, emotional, mental, and spiritual well-being? If we could answer that question we would know what to do, and it would involve something far different from "just say no" and "lock 'em up and throw away the key."

Gun Control

Denying easy access to guns and ammunition needs to be high on our national agenda. Federal control is crucial, since differing state laws make it possible to buy guns in states with weak controls and transport them across state lines. Because of the political difficulty of an outright ban on already purchased weapons, it may be necessary to impose sharp limits on the manufacture, import, and selling of ammunition. This would eventually have a major impact on gun violence.

State Killing

Like gun control and drug policy, the death penalty is a highly controversial and emotional issue. For Christians, however, there should be no dispute on this subject. There are many reasons to be against killing by the state: its inherent race and class discrimination; the inevitable execution of innocent persons; the high financial cost (several times greater than life in prison); the harm it does to the grieving and healing process for the families of both murder victims and death-row prisoners. But for those who follow Jesus, himself a victim of crime and capital punishment, there need be only one reason: that we cannot honestly imagine Jesus' participating in or condoning an execution. If we cannot conceive of Jesus' pulling the switch, or injecting the lethal needle, or pounding the nails into the hands and feet of, say, Barabbas, then—as members of a democratic society—we cannot legitimately support the death penalty. Like private one-on-one murder, legal murder is absolutely anti-restorative, bringing no healing, and reconciling no one to self, God, or anyone else.

Life Without Parole

Life without parole, or LWOP, is in one respect similar to the death penalty: we are playing God by assuming that a person cannot change—something we say we believe God would never do. Certainly there are persons who have committed vicious acts and who should never walk the streets again. But we do not know at the point of sentencing who these persons are. A restorative perspective restrains a violent offender as long as necessary, while working constructively with that offender until it is assumed that he/she is no longer dangerous to the lives of others—should that time ever come. So, while in first-degree murder cases parole should be tightly and carefully controlled, it must remain a possibility.

Hate Crimes

Many, outraged by crimes motivated by hatred of a person's race, gender, religion, disability, age, or sexual orientation, assume that such crimes can be deterred if we ratchet up the level of punishment. While such moral outrage is understandable and has the potential for constructive action, the proposed solution has many problems.

It is unreasonable, for instance, to believe that a would-be "hate criminal" who is undeterred by a possible thirty-year prison sentence would be persuaded not to commit the crime if the sentence were forty years, instead. It is equally unlikely that such a person would be deterred if the maximum sentence were to be death instead of life imprisonment. Many such people are so full of bitterness or the desire for notoriety and fame that no punishment would make them turn back.

According to such hate crime legislation, the degree of value we attribute to the victimized person is demonstrated by the degree of pain we inflict on the victimizer. Restorative justice, on the other hand, suggests that we give greater value to victims' lives and dignity by inviting them and/or their survivors to confront and engage their violators, hold them accountable face-to-face, and struggle together to determine what kind of restitution (not retribution) it would take to "make it right," insofar as possible.

Domestic Violence and Sex Abuse

The restorative justice movement has found it difficult to grapple with domestic violence and sexual abuse. Too many Christian pastors, usually men, have encouraged vulnerable victims of these crimes, usually women, to forgive their abusers prematurely. Similarly, too many naive advocates of restorative justice assume that victim-offender mediation *is* restorative justice, and that any case can and should be mediated. Cases of sexual abuse and domestic violence, however, are notoriously resistant to successful mediation, and often result in "settlement" and "reconciliation" that is premature because of complex interpersonal dynamics and what is usually a vast difference in power between victim and victimizer. For most such cases, neither long-term imprisonment nor simple mediation is a likely solution. As in addiction disorders (which often play a role in domestic violence), long-term treatment and education of abusers—and sometimes treatment of victims—is usually necessary for changes in behavior and the possibility of reconciliation.

Megan's Law

For sex offenders who are released into the community, all fifty states in the United States have a version of "Megan's Law," which mandates or allows criminal justice authorities to provide public notification to the community of the identities and whereabouts of sex abusers. Again, the very legitimate rationale is concern for public safety, while a likely additional motive may be revenge. A 2001 state Supreme Court ruling in a New Jersey case tried to balance these concerns against concerns for confidentiality in juvenile cases by setting an age range of perpetrators (up to fourteen years old) with a possible exemption when they reach eighteen. The larger question, of course, is how to balance the public safety issue with a commitment to restorative justice. The "jury"—i.e., the American people—is still out on this one.

Prison Chaplaincy

For church folk, a major criminal justice issue crying out for honest, creative attention is the place of prison ministry. Government-employed chaplaincy has recently been challenged—in some cases by states unwilling to pay for government chaplains, in others by observers of and participants in prison ministry who question the principles underlying state-funded chaplaincy. It has been the dominant model for providing some religious services, as well as recruiting and coordinating other services provided by groups from the community.

Some argue that the system is structurally inadequate in several respects: 1) By giving churches an excuse to do nothing themselves, it fosters in them an irresponsible hands-off posture. 2) It compromises chaplains' ability to gain the trust, confidence, and respect of prisoners. 3) It renders chaplains virtually powerless to confront perceived prison abuses without high risk of dismissal. To the extent that they exist, these structural flaws—which can limit both the pastoral and the prophetic dimensions of ministry in a prison context—have their effect no matter how much faith, commitment, skill, and integrity an individual chaplain may have. Conversely, many state chaplains say they can uphold prisoners' rights and humane treatment most effectively by quiet persuasion from within the system. Furthermore, they suggest that in the few states in which state employees have been replaced by prison ministers from the private sector on contract with the state, the clergy have tended to be evangelically oriented fundamentalists with an extremely narrow vision of their ministry in such a setting.

The integrity of prison ministry, as such, demands that the churches—especially the United Methodist Church with its historic Wesleyan commitment to ministry in the prisons—strengthen and revitalize the calling and the profession of prison ministry, and of the church itself, by forging creative solutions to these structural obstacles to the exercise of faithful, effective prison ministry.

An Emerging Coalition for Change

What will it take to transform the present retributive, punitive U.S. system of criminal justice into a collaborative, restorative system that encourages truth-telling, dialogue, repentance, accountability, and healing? And what will it take for us to take seriously a community's responsibility to address the root causes of crime? It is my conviction that only a growing restorative justice movement outside that system—rooted in faith communities, low-income and working-class neighborhoods, and informal groups of justice professionals—will be able to develop a strong enough political base and sufficient political consciousness to have a real impact on the present system.

The United Methodist Church, working with other religious groups and community organizations, can play a critical role. We United Methodists are to be found almost everywhere in this land. We are ethnically diverse. We have many congregations. We claim a gospel of justice and reconciliation. Surely we can be an integral part of an interfaith and grassroots movement to create, alongside our nation's bankrupt retributive system of justice, a new, alternative system based on principles of restorative justice. This would include prison and jail ministry, to be sure, but also ministry with victims, as well as with those who work in the present system. And, if it is to be distinctively restorative, it must bring victims and offenders together, face-to-face, to work out their differences as far as possible, even in serious cases. In the current cultural and political climate, even though it makes profound sense from both a practical and a spiritual, biblical standpoint, this is risky business.

One reason for this situation is that we have allowed the media, much of the legal profession, and some cynical politicians fool us into thinking that victims and offenders are separate groups of people with nothing in common. The adversarial justice system parallels the American dualism that divides us all into good people and bad people, winners and losers. If this goes unchallenged, "victims' rights" will continue to be about vengeance; advocacy for prisoners will continue to be seen by many as anti-victim; and the adversarial system will continue to reign supreme. People need to understand that ambiguity is a part of life. They need to recognize that there is common ground between victims and victimizers (as well as significant overlap, since most criminals have also been victims).

Some people can learn this in our churches if they have bold preachers. But most of us learn best through personal experience. That is why communities of faith, neighborhood associations, and worker groups need to create centers for victim-offender mediation; for settlement of community disputes; for peer mediation and conflict resolution in schools; and for neighborhood justice. It is why significant numbers of people need to become involved as volunteer mediators, trainers, and staff members. The more people who can participate in an alternative, restorative experience of justice, like mediation, family group conferencing, or sentencing circles, the sooner we will have a critical mass of persons who will no longer settle for the failed retributive system.

To make this vision real, restorative justice programs and agencies—whether United Methodist, ecumenical, interfaith, or secular—must see themselves as more than providers of mediation services. And they must see the victims and offenders whose lives they touch as more than recipients of their services. Such programs must begin to recognize those who have had this experience of alternative restorative justice as a potential constituency to be educated, organized, and mobilized into a political force for changing the retributive system into a more restorative one. Crime victims and offenders who have had the opportunity to work things out together, who have had a glimpse of a more healing system, can be major allies as we work together toward new ways of responding to conflict, crime, and violence.

It is not enough for United Methodists and others to start more and more victim-offender reconciliation programs and to mediate increasing numbers of cases, expecting the current punitive system to transform itself into the restorative justice system of our dreams. The retributive system will not be transformed without a major political struggle. That system is a political reality, rooted in certain arrangements through which powerful corporate interests and the politicians whose campaign funds and electoral prospects they control, work hand in hand.

With a powerful array of political and corporate interests determined to keep our punitive criminal justice system as it is, those of us in prison or victim ministry, and in ministries of restorative justice, will need to enter the political arena if we hope, gradually, to bring the crime-and-punishment beast to its knees. United Methodists and their allies in low-income and ethnic and minority communities can engage in this political struggle even as they help to build strong, humane, and fair models of restorative justice that might eventually replace the retributive system.

Restorative justice is all about relationships. To the extent that we, as the body of Christ, are able and willing to identify more closely with those most deeply hurt by the "principalities and powers" of our time and place—to that extent can we play a critical role not in perpetuating our current system of criminal justice, but in transforming it.

B I B L I O G R A P H Y

The Criminal Justice System and the Prison Industrial Complex

Askew, Glorya, and Gayraud Wilmore, eds. *Reclamation of Black Prisoners: A Challenge to the African American Church.* Atlanta: The ITC Press, 1993.

Bergner, Daniel. *God of the Rodeo: The Search for Hope, Faith, and a Six-Second Ride in Louisiana's Angola Prison.* New York: Crown Publishers, Inc., 1998.

Cole, David. *No Equal Justice: Race and Class in the American Criminal Justice System.* New York: The New Press, 1999.

Currie, Elliott. *Crime and Punishment in America.* New York: Metropolitan Books, 1998.

Donziger, Steven R., ed. *The Real War on Crime: The Report of the National Criminal Justice Commission.* New York: HarperCollins Publishers, 1996.

Lichtenstein, Alexander C., and Michael Kroll, with Rachel Kamel, ed. *The Fortress Economy: The Economic Role of the U.S. Prison System.* Philadelphia: American Friends Service Committee, 1990.

Miller, Jerome G. *Search and Destroy: African-American Males in the Criminal Justice System.* Cambridge, United Kingdom: Cambridge University Press, 1996.

"Prison Ministry and Restorative Justice," *Response.* New York: General Board of Global Ministries, The United Methodist Church, vol. 31, no. 6, June 1999.

Reiman, Jeffrey. *The Rich Get Richer and the Poor Get Prison: Ideology, Class and Criminal Justice.* Boston: Allyn and Bacon, 2001.

Rideau, Wilbert, and Ron Wikberg. *Life Sentences: Rage and Survival Behind Bars.* New York: Times Books, 1992.

Rubin, Edward L., ed. *Minimizing Harm: A New Crime Policy for Modern America.* Boulder: Westview Press, 1999.

Sarabi, Brigette, and Edwin Bender. *The Prison Payoff.* Portland: Western States Center & Western Prison Project, 2000.

Stern, Vivien. *A Sin Against the Future: Imprisonment in the World.* Boston: Northeastern University Press, 1998.

Taylor, Mark Lewis. *The Executed God: The Way of the Cross in Lockdown America*. Minneapolis: Fortress Press, 2001.

Wilmore, Gayraud, ed. *Black Men in Prison: The Response of the African American Church*. Atlanta: The ITC Press, 1990.

Wimsatt, William Upski. *No More Prisons*. New York: Subway and Elevated Books, 1999.

The Death Penalty

Bedau, Hugo Adam, ed. *The Death Penalty in America*. Oxford: Oxford University Press, 1982.

Haas, Kenneth C., and James A. Inciardi, eds. *Challenging Capital Punishment: Legal and Social Science Approaches*. Newbury Park: Sage Publications, Inc., 1988.

Hanks, Gardner C. *Against The Death Penalty: Christian and Secular Arguments Against Capital Punishment*. Scottdale, PA: Herald Press, 1997.

House, H. Wayne, and John Howard Yoder. *The Death Penalty Debate*. Dallas: Word Publishing, 1991.

Jackson, Jesse. *Legal Lynching: Racism, Injustice and the Death Penalty*. New York: Marlowe and Co., 1996.

Johnson, Robert. *Condemned to Die: Life Under Sentence of Death*. Prospect Heights: Waveland Press, Inc., 1989.

Lifton, Robert Jay, and Greg Mitchell. *Who Owns Death?: Capital Punishment, the American Conscience, and the End of Executions*. New York: HarperCollins Publishers, 2000.

Masur, Louis P. *Rites of Execution: Capital Punishment and the Transformation of American Culture, 1776-1865*. New York: Oxford University Press, 1989.

Megivern, James J. *The Death Penalty: An Historical and Theological Survey*. New York: Paulist Press, 1997.

Redekop, Vernon W. *A Life for a Life: The Death Penalty on Trial*. Scottdale, PA: Herald Press, 1990.

Sarat, Austin, ed. *The Killing State: Capital Punishment in Law, Politics, and Culture*. New York: Oxford University Press, 1999.

Stassen, Glen H., ed. *Capital Punishment: A Reader*. Cleveland: The Pilgrim Press, 1998.

Trombley, Stephen. *The Execution Protocol: Inside America's Capital Punishment Industry*.

New York: Anchor Books, 1992.

Von Drehle, David. *Among the Lowest of the Dead: Inside Death Row*. New York: Fawcett Crest, 1995.

Whitman, Claudia, and Julie Zimmerman, eds. Frontiers of Justice: Volume 1: *The Death Penalty*. Brunswick: Biddle Publishing Co., 1997.

Forgiveness

Jones, L. Gregory. *Embodying Forgiveness: A Theological Analysis*. Grand Rapids: William B. Eerdmans Publishing Company, 1995.

Patton, John. *Is Human Forgiveness Possible?: A Pastoral Care Perspective*. Nashville: Abingdon Press, 1985.

Shriver, Donald W. *An Ethic For Enemies: Forgiveness in Politics*. New York: Oxford University Press, 1995.

Tutu, Desmond. *No Future Without Forgiveness*. New York: Doubleday, 1999.

Restorative Justice

Bazemore, Gordon, and Lode Walgrave. *Restorative Juvenile Justice: Repairing the Harm of Youth Crime*. Monsey, NY: Criminal Justice Press, 1999.

Denison, Kathleen. *Restoring Justice in Ourselves*. Akron, PA: Mennonite Central Committee, U. S. Office of Criminal Justice, issue no. 11, 1991.

Hudson, Joe, and Allison Morris; Gabrielle Maxwell and Burt Galaway, eds. *Family Group Conferences: Perspectives on Policy and Practice*. Monsey, NY: The Federation Press, 1996.

Mackey, Virginia. *Restorative Justice: Toward Nonviolence*. Louisville: Presbyterian Church (U.S.A.), 1997.

Pepinsky, Harold E., and Richard Quinney, eds. *Criminology as Peacemaking*. Bloomington: Indiana University Press, 1991.

"The Phenomenon of Restorative Justice," *Contemporary Justice Review,* Sullivan, Dennis, ed.; Larry Tifft and Peter Cordella, assoc. eds. Newark: Gordon and Breach Publishers, vol. 1, no. 1, 1998.

The Restorative Justice and Mediation Collection. Published by Center for Restorative Justice and Peacemaking, University of Minnesota, on a grant from the Office for Victims of Crime,

U. S. Department of Justice, April 2000.

Umbreit, Mark S. *Crime and Reconciliation: Creative Options for Victims and Offenders*. Nashville: Abingdon Press, 1985.

Van Ness, Daniel W., and Karen Heetderks Strong. *Restoring Justice*. Cincinnati: Anderson Publishing Company, 1997.

Zehr, Howard. *Changing Lenses: A New Focus for Crime and Justice*. Scottdale, PA: Herald Press, 1995.

Mediating the Victim-Offender Conflict: The Victim-Offender Reconciliation Program. Elkhart, IN: Mennonite Central Committee, 1990.

Restorative Justice: International Dimensions

Galaway, Burt, and Joe Hudson, eds. *Restoring Justice: International Perspectives*. Monsey, NY: Criminal Justice Press, 1996.

Herr, Robert, and Judy Zimmerman Herr, eds. *Transforming Violence: Linking Local and Global Peacemaking*. Scottdale, PA: Herald Press, 1998.

Krog, Antjie. *Country of My Skull: Guilt, Sorrow, and the Limits of Forgiveness in the New South Africa*. New York: Three Rivers Press, 2000.

Mulunda-Nyanga, Ngoy Daniel. *The Reconstruction of Africa: Faith and Freedom for a Conflicted Continent*. Nairobi, Kenya: All Africa Council, 1997.

"Restorative Justice Worldwide," *New World Outlook*. New York: General Board of Global Ministries, The United Methodist Church, vol. 59, no. 6, July-August 1999.

Ross, Rupert. *Returning to the Teachings: Exploring Aboriginal Justice*. Toronto: Penguin Books, 1996.

Ressler, Lawrence, and Carolyn Schrock-Shenk, eds. *Making Peace with Conflict: Practical Skills for Conflict Transformation*. Scottdale, Pa.: Herald Press, 1999.

Theological Perspectives

"The Church and the Criminal Justice System," *Church and Society Journal*. National Ministries Division, Presbyterian Church (U.S.A.), vol. 87, no. 4., March-April 1997.

Griffith, Lee. *The Fall of the Prison: Biblical Perspectives on Prison Abolition*. Grand Rapids: William B. Eerdmans Publishing Company, 1993.

Mackey, Virginia. *Punishment: In the Scripture and Tradition of Judaism, Christianity and Islam.* Published by Presbyterian Church (U. S. A.), 1981.

Raphael, Pierre. *Inside Rikers Island: A Chaplain's Search for God.* New York: Orbis Books, 1990.

Snyder, T. Richard. *The Protestant Ethic and the Spirit of Punishment.* Grand Rapids: William B. Eerdmans Publishing Company, 2001.

Victimization and Crime

Arnold, B. Hope. *Respect, Reconciliation: A Christian Response to Gun Violence.* Louisville: Presbyterian Church (U.S.A.), 1996.

Delaplane, D., and A. Delaplane. *Victims of Child Abuse, Domestic Violence, Elderly Abuse, Rape, Robbery, Assault, Violent Death: A Manual for Clergy and Congregations.* Denver: The Spiritual Dimension in Victims Series.

Dicks, Shirley. *Victims of Crime and Punishment: Interviews with Victims, Convicts, Their Families, and Support Groups.* Jefferson, NC: McFarland and Company, Inc., Publishers, 1991.

Elias, Robert. *The Politics of Victimization: Victims, Victimology and Rights.* New York: Oxford University Press, 1986.

Fortune, Marie M. *Sexual Violence: The Unmentionable Sin, An Ethical and Pastoral Perspective.* New York: Pilgrim Press, 1983.

——. *Keeping the Faith: Questions and Answers for the Abused Woman.* San Francisco: Harper and Row Publishers, 1987.

——. *Violence in the Family: A Workshop Curriculum for Clergy and Other Helpers.* Cleveland: The Pilgrim Press, 1991.

Lampman, Lisa Barnes, ed., with Michelle D. Shattuck, assoc. ed. *God and the Victim: Theological Reflections on Evil, Victimization, Justice, and Forgiveness.* Grand Rapids: William B. Eerdmans Publishing Company, 1999.

New Directions from the Field: Victims' Rights and Services for the 21st Century. U. S. Department of Justice. Washington D.C., 2000.

Strategies for Implementation, Tools for Action Guide: Victims' Rights and Services for the 21st Century. U. S. Department of Justice. Washington D.C., 2000.

Wilkinson, Henrietta, and William Arnold. *Victims of Crime: A Christian Perspective.* Louisville: Presbyterian Church (U.S.A.), 1990.

Women and the Criminal Justice System

Bauschard, Louise, with Mary Kimbrough. *Voices Set Free: Battered Women Speak from Prison*. St. Louis: Women's Self Help Center, 1986.

Bloom, Barbara, Russ Immarigeon, and Barbara Owen, eds. *The Prison Journal: Women in Prisons and Jails*. Thousand Oaks, CA.: Sage Periodicals Press, vol. 75, no. 2, June 1995.

Culhane, Charles, special ed. *Concrete Garden: Women and the Criminal Justice System*. New York: Buffalo Group on Justice in Democracy, vol. 4, 1996.

Harlow, Barbara. *Barred: Women, Writing, and Political Detention.* Hanover: Wesleyan University Press, 1992.

Harris, Jean. *Stranger in Two Worlds*. New York: Kensington Publishing Corporation, 1986.

Madriz, Esther. *Nothing Bad Happens to Good Girls: Fear of Crime in Women's Lives*. Berkeley: University of California Press, July 1997.

Shea, Kathleen. *Women on the Row: Revelations from Both Sides of the Bars.* Ithaca: Firebrand Books, 2000.

Yoder, Elizabeth G., ed. *Peace Theology and Violence Against Women*. Occasional Papers, no. 16. Elkhart, IN: Institute of Mennonite Studies, 1992.

Videography

A Journey of Hope: From Violence to Healing. 11 min. Kindheart Films, 3000 Windemere Circle, Nashville, TN 37214, 615-872-0243.

America's Failed War on Drugs: Shadow Conventions 2000. 48 min. Lindesmith Center, 4455 Connecticut Avenue, NW, no. B-500, Washington, D.C. 20008, 202-537-5005.

Cool Hand Luke. 127 min. Gordon Carroll, producer. Stuart Rosenberg, director. Warner Brothers. 1967.

Corrections. 58 minutes. Ashley Hunt and Jonas Hudson, producers. Ashley Hunt, director. Info_corrections@yahoo.com, 718-791-5500. 2000.

Dead Man Walking. 122 min. Tim Robbins, director. 1996.

The Farm: Life Inside Angola Prison. 100 min. Jonathan Stack and Liz Garbus, producers and directors. Michael Cascio, executive producer. Gabriel Films for A&E Network. 1998.

Fisk University Race Relations Institute Presents Dr. Angela Davis@Critical Resistance: Beyond the Prison Industrial Complex, November 16, 1998. 1000 17th Avenue, North, Nashville, TN 37208. 615-329-8525. Rwinbush@usit.net.

Prisoner Visitation and Support—Reaching Beyond Prison Bars: A Nationwide Alternative Ministry to Federal and Military Prisoners. 21 min. Eric Corson, PVS, 1501 Cherry Street, Philadelphia, PA 19102, 215-241-7117.

Restorative Justice: Victim Empowerment Through Mediation and Dialogue. 25 min. Center for Restorative Justice and Mediation, School of Social Work, St. Paul, MN.

Restoring Justice. 51 min. Produced for the National Council of the Churches of Christ in the USA, by the Presbyterian Church (U.S.A.), 100 Witherspoon St., Louisville, KY. 40202-1396. 1996.

The Shawshank Redemption. 142 min. Liz Glotzer and David Lester, executive producers. Frank Darabont, director. Castle Rock Entertainment. 1994.

Yes, In My Backyard. 57 min. Tracy Huling, producer, in association with WSKG Public Broadcasting. Galloping Girls Productions, Inc., R.R. 1, Box 168, Freehold, NY 12431.

S T U D Y   G U I D E

by Brenda Connelly

INTRODUCTION

For I know the plans I have for you, says the Lord,
plans for welfare and not for evil, to give you a future and a hope.

(Jeremiah 29:11)

On Friday night, in a maximum security prison, a group of men met to read and discuss the great books. The next evening, some volunteers came for a time of fellowship. Both meetings took place in the prison chapel. It was one of those Saturday evening fellowship groups that I attended some twenty-five years ago. I was invited by one of the regular volunteers, and went with much fear and trepidation. On the drive to the prison I kept thinking, "I'll go this once, then say it's not for me, and I won't have to go back again." Upon our arrival, we assembled with some twelve to fifteen other volunteers and began our walk to the chapel through one clanging door after another. My anxieties grew. Finally after twisting and turning down several long corridors, through a series of steel-bar gates, and up and down numerous flights of stairs, we arrived at the chapel, somewhere deep within the prison complex.

Twenty men were waiting for us . What I saw was very young men with expressions that registered no hope. For me, it was a life-changing experience. I began an engagement with the criminal justice system that led me back into the prisons several times each week for more than ten years.

As I continued my visits, I wondered about the people I visited:

- What had happened in their lives that caused them to end up in prison?

- Could something have been done earlier in their lives to prevent their becoming offenders of society, rather than what we consider productive citizens?

- What would their futures be upon their release?

Early on, I met a young man whom I'll call Luke. He came from the inner city. Excelling in school was not popular in his neighborhood, nor was it a concern of his family. He had purposely not done well in school, and had eventually dropped out. At the age of eighteen he had ended up in prison. Like most of his fellow prisoners he was undereducated. But, while in prison, he took advantage of every educational opportunity that presented itself. He worked as a tutor with the Laubach program (based on the principle of "each one teach one"), teaching other inmates how to read. Upon completion of the program, they would be reading at fifth-grade level, which is considered functionally literate. Luke was a member of the Great Books group. He completed his GED, received a college degree, and began work on his masters. In the prison he was seen as a strong leader who could overcome many obstacles, and someone who would have no problems upon release on parole.

Finally came the day of his release. He walked out the front gate and headed for the university where he had a teaching fellowship. Luke had made it. But had he? As much as he had achieved in prison, he was now faced with new obstacles and challenges. His family and friends back in the city made fun of him and scoffed at him for being educated and too good to associate with them. Nor did he fit in with the world of academia. Luke had spent the years from his late teens to his early thirties in prison, missing the normal experiences of socialization as one moves from one's teens into adulthood. Where did he fit in? It has not been easy for Luke to "stay clean." He has had many struggles with reintegration into society.

As I continued my involvement with prisons, I became more actively engaged with the women. Over and over again, they told me stories of physical and sexual abuse. Often these were also stories of their mothers. I asked myself: How do we break these cycles of abuse? How do we enable women, in particular, to have the inner strength, and how do we provide them with the financial support and protection to move out of abusive situations into a safe environment? And what about the children? How do we break the cycle of violence so they will be prevented from following their parent(s) to prison?

But restorative justice is about more than jails and prisons. Crime points to the voids and inequities in our society. Restorative justice is about its harmony and wholeness. It is about right relationships and equity for everyone—for all of God's children. It is hope for the homeless, help for the abused, and work for a better tomorrow. How do we respond to a society that says it is okay to charge the poor as much as 2000 percent for a quick "payday" loan from a check-cashing outlet, for industry to pollute the air, and for slum landlords to gouge the poor, while it locks up the shoplifter and the drug user? How do we make salaries more equitable so that everyone will have the means to support a family and have a decent home? How do we change a system that discriminates against the poor into one that gives them a future and hope?

AS YOU PREPARE FOR THIS STUDY

Using This Study Guide

It is important to remember and to tell your group that you are the study leader, not the teacher, and that you will all be learning from one another. The purpose of this guide is to assist you in leading group participants to explore the materials in the text, as well as supplementary resources, to gain an understanding of restorative justice. Along with the text you are encouraged to use *Response* and *New World Outlook* magazines as primary resources.

1. As you prepare for this study, it is important to ground it biblically. We begin the first session with Bible study, and continue in the sessions that follow.

2. Building community with the class is important as you begin. There will be participants from a variety of backgrounds and experiences. You will need to establish trust and openness to different points of view.

3. A variety of teaching methods is used throughout this guide. Several activities are designed for small groups. My personal preference is to allow people to form into groups as they choose (you set the limit on the number per group), and then continue working in that group. You may wish to encourage them to take turns as leaders within their small groups and as presenters to the class.

4. Create two outlines for your class sessions:
    a. One is detailed, with anticipated lengths of time for each section. This is *your* outline. Be prepared with an optional learning activity in the event that something takes less time than allotted, or if something really doesn't work with your group.

    b. The second is a condensed outline for *group participants*. Do not include times, since if you are running late with an activity, participants tend to get hung up on time rather than focusing on content.

5. Encourage additional reading. For those who participate in the reading program of United Methodist Women, several of the books cited here are on the reading list.

6. It is important to make assignments for the study at the end of the first session. If the study is to be done in a one-day setting, try to assign people who you know will be coming, to be prepared with specific presentations.

PREPARING THE ROOM

Create an environment of learning by placing posters and pictures around the room. The building of a collage, as suggested in the introduction to Session 1, can be a part of this. Have a table with clearly marked resources for browsing only, as well as hand-outs that can be taken to keep. Seating, either in a semi-circle or at tables, should be arranged in such a way that everyone can see and hear everyone else. This is particularly important for group discussions.

1

READING FOR THIS SESSION

Chapters 1 and 2

Goal

To examine our attitudes toward crime and punishment, and to reflect on the biblical perspective surrounding restorative justice

Supplies

Newsprint, felt-tip markers, masking tape, ball of yarn, glue stick, colored paper, name tags, Bibles (at least 3), signs with the words "Strongly Agree" and "Strongly Disagree" for Continuum, copies for each group participant of handouts for Session 1, copy of text, *Response* and *New World Outlook* issues for this study, *Global Praise 1*, copies of appropriate handouts for assignments you will be making at the end of this class

Getting Acquainted

Getting Connected: This activity is to help with connecting names and faces. Say your name and where you are from as you throw the ball of yarn to someone in the class, holding on to the loose end. Ask each group member, in turn, holding on to the yarn, to throw the ball to someone else. Then it will be that person's turn to tell her/his name and hometown, state, or country, and throw the ball to someone else. Continue until everyone in the room is connected.

As We Begin: Before the first class, on a large sheet of newsprint write "Restorative justice means_____" and post it on the wall. As people arrive, have colored paper and markers near the door. Ask each person to write a word or phrase on a sheet of paper, completing that statement. When all are finished, ask them to introduce themselves to the group and read out loud what they have written. As they do this, ask them to glue what they have written on the sheet of newsprint.

Personal Inventory

As we begin this study, let us first reflect on our own perceptions regarding our justice system. What are our feelings about prisons, victims, and society's responsibility? As you read the Bible, what directives do you consider important? The following statements are for your personal response. Complete each one as we prepare to begin this study. They are for your personal reflection only, and you will be asked to look at them again from time to time during the course of this study.

1. People in prison generally belong to the following groups: _____.

2. The purpose of our prisons is _____.

3. Most victims of crime belong to the following groups: _____.

4. I believe that restitution means _____.

5. When I think of justice, I think of _____.

6. Regarding violators of the law, the Bible says _____.

Meditation

Scripture: Isaiah 32:16-18

Hymn "Help us to be peace-makers" *Global Praise* 1, No. 29

Prayer:

God, our Creator, we ask you to guide us as we begin to struggle with what it means to be "peace-makers" in a society in which violence on television is accepted as normal, and exploitation of the poor is not regarded as our concern. Forgive us for our lack of forgiveness for the offender and our shunning of the victim. Give us the courage to stand up for our convictions when we are needed, and to speak out even though it may not be popular. Amen.

As We Continue

We cannot turn on the news or pick up a newspaper without reading about the latest rape, murder, or robbery in our community. Sometimes we may read and hear about the same one for several days. We are afraid. We want to be protected from the possibility of such violation. Frequently society's "solution" is sentencing the violator to prison—a specific process for dealing with crime and punishment. It has been a major part of our society and felt needed by people for various reasons—protection, security, fear, reform, punishment. (Such arrangements are usually referred to as correctional, prison, or criminal justice systems.) There are some who feel that the primary purpose of a jail or prison is to bring about change in the person who has committed a violation against someone else. Others think it is a means of punishing an offender for wrongdoing. And still others, out of frustration and a sense of hopelessness, see no alternative to locking up the perpetrators (or having them executed) to stop them from doing it again—at least for now. What are we doing, and to what end?

In recent years we have seen the building of more and more prisons and jails—often at the expense of education. People are being sentenced to prison for longer terms without a chance of parole. We are seeing children and teens being treated as adults and thrown into adult prisons in an attempt to protect society. But what caused a child to commit murder in the first place? Could we have done something much earlier to prevent this tragedy? What guidance does the gospel give for our response to victim as well as victimizer? And why are so many people striking out with such violence?

Begin by giving your group an overview of the course and some idea of how you will proceed as study leader. Call attention to the primary resources you will use, as well as supplemental reading. Be sure to include *Response* and *New World Outlook* magazines.

Bible Study

It is important, as we begin, to be serious about our examination of the biblical base and the centuries of tradition that will guide us in the search for a perspective on justice. We struggle with the stories of violence—particularly in the Old Testament (or Hebrew Scriptures)—as well as those of forgiveness and peace. There are stories of brokenness as well as of healing. How do they speak to us today as we talk about restorative justice? It is important to understand that we are talking about more than incarceration. Restorative justice is healing for the victim, the community, and the victimizer. It's the forming of right relationships.

In the introduction to the text, the author gives a brief overview of crime and punishment, both central to the Bible and our faith. He concludes with the statement, "[I]t is an invitation to discipleship, offering a way to walk with Jesus within a community of faith and witness dedicated to his vision of ministry with the victims (Luke 10:25-37), hospitable presence with those in prison (Matthew 25:31-46), and liberty to the captives (Isaiah 61:1-2 and Luke 4:16-30)."

Discussion

Divide participants into three groups and ask them to discuss the assigned Scripture passage, then write their responses on newsprint and report back to the whole group.

Group 1: Luke 10:25-37

1. Can the actions of the priest and the Levite be justified?

2. With whom do you identify most strongly in this story? How? Why?

3. How does this passage relate to restorative justice?

Group 2: Matthew 25:31-46

1. Are there others besides those mentioned in this passage that might be considered "the least of these"?

2. What does this passage say to you about restorative justice?

Group 3: Isaiah 61:1-2, Luke 4:16-30

1. We are challenged by these passages to work in five areas. If all five are to be addressed, which area of concern has your undivided attention and which may be put on the back burner? Why?

2. Do you think these five areas are being addressed today in terms of restorative justice?

Continuum

Before the group meets, place two signs— *Strongly Agree* and *Strongly Disagree*—on opposite sides of the room. Tell group members that you will read a statement. They are to move next to one sign or the other, or anywhere between those two points, in order to express their position. After reading each statement, ask participants to state why they took the stand they did. If they are positioned in different places, which is more than likely, ask for a response from someone in each grouping. Here are the statements:

1. Most people in prison deserve to be there.

2. While prisons are not the solution to all our problems, they offer the best way to protect society.

3. Making drug treatment centers more readily available to addicts is an alternative that would cut down on the number sent to prison and help addicts turn their lives around.

Assignments

Reading for Session 2: Chapters 3 and 4

Assign two teams of volunteers to make preparations for the debate to be presented in Session 2.

H A N D O U T   1 A

Personal Reflection

1. People in prison generally belong to the following groups: _____.

2. The purpose of our prisons is _____.

3. Most victims of crime belong to the following groups: _____.

4. I believe that restitution means _____.

5. When I think of justice, I think of _____.

6. Regarding violators of the law, the Bible says_____ .

Meditation

Scripture: Isaiah 32:16-18

Hymn: "Help us to be peace-makers" *Global Praise 1,* **No. 29**

Prayer: God, our Creator, we ask you to guide us as we begin to struggle with what it means to be "peace makers" in a society where violence on television is accepted as normal and exploitation of the poor is not regarded our concern. Forgive us for our lack of forgiveness of the offender and for our shunning of the victim. Give us courage to stand up when needed and speak out even though it may not be popular. Amen.

Bible Study

Group 1: Luke 10:25-37

1. Can the actions of the priest and the Levite be justified?

2. With whom in this story do you most identify? How?

3. What is the purpose of this Scripture passage as it relates to restorative justice?

Group 2: Matthew 25:31-46

1. Are there others besides those mentioned in this passage that might be considered "the least of these"?

2. What does this say to you about restorative justice?

Group 3: Isaiah 61:1-2 and Luke 4:16-30

1. We are challenged through these passages to work in five areas. If all five are to be addressed, which area of concern gets your undivided attention and which area may be put on the back burner? Why?

2. Do you see this being done today in relationship to restorative justice?

2

READING FOR THIS SESSION

Chapters 3 and 4

Goal

To begin exploring and defining the differences between retributive justice and restorative justice

Preparation

- Copies of *The United Methodist Hymnal*, copies of Handouts 2A and 2B, poster with definitions of retributive and restorative justice, enough 3"x 5" cards in two different colors for all group members

- Set up table for debaters in front of room. Have a designated chair for the timekeeper. Have available the following: newsprint, markers, masking tape, Bibles, copies of *New World Outlook*, Social Principles (in either *The Book of Discipline of The United Methodist Church* or *The Book of Resolutions of The United Methodist Church*), relevant material about restorative justice from the Internet, newspaper articles, and current periodicals.

- Have table (preferably small), teapot, and two cups as props for the skit *Called to Go*.

- Four sheets of newsprint with the following headings:

  1. Root Causes of Crime and Violence

  2. Responses Based on Biblical Principles

  3. Responses Based on Wesleyan Tradition

  4. Responses Based on Restorative Justice

The first will be used at the end of "Looking at the Facts." The others will be used at the end of the skit. Have them ready to post on the wall. (When writing on newsprint taped to the wall, be sure it doesn't bleed through onto wall. Use double sheets, if necessary.)

Definitions

Retributive justice defines crime as breaking the law of the state and owing a "debt to society."

Restorative justice defines crime as one person or organization violating another and owing a debt to the victim and, secondly, to the local community.

Meditation

Distribute Handout 2A

Scripture: Leviticus 19:15; Matthew 5:43-48

Prayer in Unison: "For Courage to Do Justice," *The United Methodist Hymnal*, No. 456

Hymn: "Open My Eyes, That I May See," *The United Methodist Hymnal*, No. 454

Looking at the Facts

As we continue this study, it is important to look at the statistics in order to help our understanding of who is affected by the criminal justice system and whether it is truly a just system for all people. There are many myths as well as a considerable lack of knowledge throughout the penal system as to who is affected and what difference that system makes—both positive and negative.

Following are statements to use in reviewing the text for this session. You may have other statements that you wish to add or substitute. As you read them, ask group members to respond by holding up their cards of colored paper: one color if they are aware of this information; the other color if the statement is new information to them; both cards if they have no idea one way or the other. (Post cards with corresponding definitions for everyone to see.) This is another way of allowing everyone to participate. The statements are direct quotes from Chapter 1 of the text. Group members may wish to check the text for more information after you have read the statements and allowed the class to respond.

1. "The United States imprisons a higher percentage of its people than any other nation in the world . . . ."

2. "The smallest group [of prisoners] by far—approximately 1 percent—consists of white-collar, corporate criminals."

3. "Of the 1.4 million in state prisons in 1998, approximately 135,000 were murderers; 100,000 were sex offenders; and 160 armed robber—crimes that fit the stereotype of violent predators, adding up to roughly 35 percent of all prisoners. Most of the others were there for offenses related to property, public order, and drugs."

4. "Today's U.S. prison population is 49 percent African-American and 18 percent Hispanic. . . .When Native Americans and Asian Americans are factored in as well, the states with the greatest disparity in the rates of incarceration of whites versus people of color are all in the Northeast and the Midwest. . . ."

5. "While African Americans constitute about 15 percent of regular illegal drug users in this country (close to their 13 percent of the national population), . . . they make up 74 percent of those incarcerated for drug possession."

6. "[T]he downsizing or closing of residential mental health hospitals . . . has been disastrous. It has led to a massive increase in homelessness, as well as dumping many mentally ill persons into the lap of a criminal justice system that is ill-prepared to deal with them humanely or effectively."

7. "Not only is juvenile crime diminishing sharply, but the currently favored solutions for the problem are, if anything, counterproductive."

8. "The annual figure for imprisoning a juvenile is . . . $35,000 (compared to $7,000 for a year of public school)."

Ask group members for their responses to this information.

■ What does this exercise tell us about the difference between perception and fact? (Sometimes there is so much emphasis on crime in the media that it is blown out of all proportion.)

■ Were there some that came as a real surprise to you? If so, which ones, and why?

■ What are some of the issues we need to address as individuals and as churches?

■ Ask group members to start a list on newsprint with the heading, "Root Causes of Crime and Violence." (This will be expanded as you move through the study.) In the last session you will look at possible ways of responding to some of these issues.

Video

View the restorative justice segment of the *Mission Magazine* video. This will give a brief overview of the study and another way to identify some of the issues.

Debate

In the first session you assigned two teams to prepare for a debate. Select one of the following two topics:

1. "Resolved: That the criminal justice system falls short in achieving its goal."

One team will take the position that the criminal justice system is achieving its goal; the other team will take the opposite position.

2. "[E]ye for eye, tooth for a tooth," (Exodus 21:23-24) vs. "Turn to him the other [cheek] also" (Matthew 5:39-41)

One team will support "an eye for an eye" with current examples and information, while the other team will do so for "turn the other cheek."

■ Use statistics and facts to support your position. Be specific.

■ Give examples to support your position.

■ Use but do not limit yourself to the following resources: *Response, New World Outlook, The Book of Resolutions of The United Methodist Church* (including the Social Principles), Appendix E (The Death Penalty), websites, and newspapers.

Allow each team five minutes to make the initial presentation supporting its position. Ask someone to serve as timekeeper. Ask group members for questions and comments. At the end, allow an additional two minutes for a rebuttal from each team.

Bible Study

The second chapter of the text begins by looking at restorative justice with a focus on accountability and healing for all. Pass out the handouts for Session 2, and ask group members to divide into three groups. Ask them to discuss the questions and assign someone to report back to the whole group. If they are working in the same groups as before, encourage them to have a different presenter.

Group 1: Matthew 21:12-13; 22:15-22

1. What do these biblical passages say about restorative justice in our own day?

2. As you reflect on these readings, what do they say to you about God's expectations of how we are to live? Give some examples.

Group 2: John 8:2-11

1. What does this say to us about punishment and forgiveness?

2. Who has been hurt and what are their needs?

3. Give some examples of how this relates to us today.

Group 3: Matthew 20:1-16

1. As you read this passage, put yourself in the place of a) the first hired, b) the last hired, 3) the employer. How did you feel in each of these positions?

2. How does this speak to restorative justice?

3. If this were to happen today, what would be the response? Give an example.

Ask each group report back to the class.

Getting Down to Basics

Ask those who have prepared the skit *Called to Go*, printed on Handout 2C, to present it to the class. After the presentation, post three sheets of newsprint beside the one labeled "Root Causes of Crime and Violence." On these, write the following headings:

a) Responses Based on Biblical Principles

b) Responses Based on Wesleyan Tradition

c) Responses Based on Restorative Justice

Ask group participants to list responses to root causes from their readings in Chapters 1 and 2 under those three areas. Suggest that they add to these lists at any time during the course of the study. This will be helpful in the last session when the group will look at ways in which we need to respond.

Assignments

Reading for Session 3: Chapter 5

Presenters of dramatic presentations based on the stories in Session 3 need to be ready.

Meditation

Scripture: Leviticus 19:15; Matthew 5:43-48

Prayer in Unison: "For Courage to Do Justice," *The United Methodist Hymnal*, No. 456

Hymn: "Open My Eyes, That I May See," *The United Methodist Hymnal*, No. 454

Bible Study

Group 1: Matthew 21:12-13; 22:15-22

1. What do these biblical passages say about restorative justice in our own day?

2. As you reflect on these readings, what do they say to you about God's expectations of how we are to live? Give some examples.

Group 2: John 8:2-11

1. What does this say to us about punishment and forgiveness?

2. Who has been hurt and what are their needs?

3. Give some examples of how this relates to us today.

Group 3: Matthew 20:1-16

1. As you read this passage, put yourself in the place of a) the first hired, b) the last hired, c) the employer. How did you feel in each of these positions?

2. How does this speak to restorative justice?

3. If this were to happen today, what would be the response? Give an example.

DEBATE

In the first session, you assigned two teams to prepare for a debate. Select one of the following two topics:

1. "Resolved: That the criminal justice system falls short in achieving its goal."

One team will take the position that the criminal justice system is achieving its goal; the other team will take the opposite position.

2. "[E]ye for eye, tooth for tooth," (Exodus 21:23-24) vs. "[T]urn to him the other [cheek] also" (Matthew 5:39-41)

One team will support "an eye for an eye" with current examples and information, while the other team will do so for "turn the other cheek."

■ Use statistics and facts to support your position. Be specific.

■ Give examples to support your position.

■ Use but do not limit yourself to the following resources: *Response, New World Outlook, The Book of Resolutions of The United Methodist Church* (including the Social Principles), Appendix E (The Death Penalty), websites, and newspapers.

Allow each team five minutes to make the initial presentation supporting its position.

Ask someone to serve as timekeeper.

Ask group members for questions and comments.

At the end, allow an additional two minutes for a rebuttal from each team.

CALLED TO GO

Scene: A room with a table, two chairs, a teapot, and two cups

Narrator: The time is about 1750, late afternoon, in England. The place is Sarah Peters's kitchen. She is having tea with her friend Mary.

Mary: Tell me, Sarah, about your going to the prisons. Why are you going there so much?

Sarah: I'm not doing this alone. You know I meet regularly with several others and John Wesley. And as we studied and prayed, we were led to be present with the people in prison and talk with them about God's grace. Mary, it's just horrible, the conditions these people are forced to live in. And for such petty reasons!

Mary: Oh, Sarah, I wouldn't want to go to prison. Those people are dangerous. They're likely to harm you!

Sarah: (shaking her head) Often those in prison are there because they can't pay back a small loan. This was just more than the Wesleys could endure. They raised the money to pay off some of these debts so these people could get out of prison.

Mary: But why help them get out? They could harm us.

Sarah: Oh Mary, Mary. We're talking about not paying back a couple of shillings. And did you know that even Charles and John Wesley's father, Samuel, actually spent time in debtor's prison? And he used to make visits in the prisons of Oxford in the 1680s when he was a student at Exeter. The Wesleys began going into the prisons to visit once or twice a week while they were at Oxford as members of the Holy Club. They believe you need to minister to the whole person—to the mental, spiritual, and physical needs of the prisoners. But they received much criticism and teasing. It hasn't stopped them, though, and they continue their visits. John says he's been called to prison ministry. He cites the parable in Matthew 25: 31-46.

Mary: Well, according to what I've heard, John's not allowed to preach from any pulpit. He sounds like someone of questionable character to me. Sarah, are you sure you should be doing this kind of thing?

Sarah: (laughing) Of course, Mary. This is exactly what I should be doing. Maybe John isn't allowed to preach in the pulpit because some of the leaders don't understand or approve of what he's doing. But, Mary, he's making such a difference in the lives of people! Let me tell you what happened to him. I think it's why he's continued going into the prisons and will as long as he lives.

Mary: (becoming interested, in spite of herself) Tell me. What did he do?

Sarah: John and Charles Wesley went as missionaries to one of the American colonies around fifteen years ago. It was a place where many English debtors had gone after they got out of prison. They went with a man named Oglethorpe. John spent two years there in a colony named Georgia, and then returned to England. It was a bad time for him. He grew more and more troubled about his soul and his faith.

Mary: (under her breath) I told you he was of questionable character.

Sarah: ignoring Mary's comment) Peter Bohler told him, "Preach faith till you have it, and then, because you have it, you will preach faith." The first time Wesley spoke of salvation by faith alone, it was to a death-sentenced prisoner named Clifford. Wesley said Clifford died "in perfect peace." And, Mary, just weeks later Wesley had his own life-changing spiritual experience. It was at a meeting on Aldersgate Street. He says that is where he finally reached the perfect peace of trust, and the assurance of forgiveness. Mary, how can we ignore these children of God who are forced to live in such deplorable conditions—often for such trivial offenses? I truly believe I'm doing what God wants and expects me to do.

Mary: Well, Sarah, I think I do have a little more understanding of why you're doing it, though I'm not sure I completely agree with you. But perhaps . . .

Sarah: Mary, why don't you have another cup of tea? (pours more tea) All I ask is that you keep an open mind as you read and pray about it. If you want to talk again, you know where to find me.

Moderator: Prison visitation was seen by John Wesley and others as so important a feature of a life of Christian discipleship that a 1778 Conference decision made it obligatory for all Methodist preachers. Bishop Kenneth Carder has reminded more recent Methodists that "the Wesleys spent much more time at [London's] Newgate Prison than at Aldersgate Street," and he even goes so far as to declare that "a case can be made that Newgate Prison (and the other prisons across England) were as decisive in sparking the Methodist revival as the experience at Aldersgate."

3

READING FOR THIS SESSION

Review Chapter 4, and read Chapter 5

Goal

To hear stories of brokenness and injustice in a global context, and then ask the following questions: Who was harmed? What are their needs? Whose obligation are they?

Preparation

Set up the room so that everyone can see the area where the open-ended stories will be presented. Have ready for distribution copies of Handouts 3A and 3B.

Meditation

Scripture: Matthew 5:43-48

Litany: *Welcome, Travelers* (see Handout 3A)

Hymn: "Where Cross the Crowded Ways of Life," *The United Methodist Hymnal,* No. 427

SETTING THE STAGE

Much of this study has focused on restorative justice issues in the United States, but they have countless global applications as well. In this session we will look at some of these justice issues as well as continue to explore those that are also issues for us in the United States. As you will remember from reading Chapter 4 for the last session, much brokenness has come from civil war, dictatorships, and totalitarianism. It tells us of the many questions being asked about the past as well as the present. Many advocates of restorative justice firmly believe that the first steps toward healing are taken when governments and civil society tell the truth about past atrocities carried out by the state.

As you listen to the following stories, put yourself in the position of the person telling the story. What are your responses?

LISTENING IN ORDER TO RESPOND

Following are five open-ended stories that tell us about brokenness. Distribute Handout A for

Session 3. Volunteers should be ready to make their presentations. After they have finished, there will be an opportunity for group members to respond to the questions on the handout. Instruct them, as they listen and watch, to put themselves in the position of one of the people named in each scenario, and to listen as that person. Then, after the dramatization, ask them to respond from the position of that person. After each story, discuss the questions on Handout 3B.

a) We found a woman. I called a soldier and I told him, "Take charge of this woman. She's a gift from the sublieutenant." "I understand, my corporal," he told me and he called the boys and said, "There's meat here, you guys." Then they came and grabbed the girl. They took her little boy away from her and all of them raped her. It was a huge gang rape. Later I told them to kill the woman before killing her son so she wouldn't feel so bad about the death of her son."

— Testimony of a perpetrator in Guatemala, 1982, from the REMHI (Recovery of Historic Memory) Report.

b) Angelina, a thirteen-year-old student, is at the top of her eighth-grade class. Her home, which is in the area of Palestine that was reoccupied, was taken over by the Israeli army and was used by the soldiers as a shooting base. Angelina and the other members of her family, all thirteen of them, were locked into one room in the house for two days and were not allowed to get food or even to go to the bathroom without the soldiers' permission. Angelina and her family are physically fine, but the memory and trauma of being taken hostage in their own house will take a long time to get over (see *Restorative Justice: Moving Beyond Punishment*, ch. 4).

The soldiers tied up every one inside the house without asking any questions. They poured gasoline on the house and set it on fire. Everyone inside died in the fire including a two-year-old child. My mother, sister and brother-in-law died along with their three children (see *Restorative Justice: Moving Beyond Punishment*, ch. 4).

c) Mrs. Lamb, who is eighty years old, has some health problems and trouble getting around. Susan, fifty-four, came to live with her. Things were going well until Susan lost her job. She has started drinking excessively and spent hours in front of the TV. This angered Mrs. Lamb and led to arguments between them. Recently, the arguments have been getting physical. Mrs. Lamb discovered that Susan has been taking large sums of money out of their joint account. Mrs. Lamb is upset and frightened that confronting Susan will make her angrier. (*Elder Abuse, Neglect, and Exploitation*, Center on Aging and Older Adult Ministries, General Board of Discipleship, The United Methodist Church, Nashville, TN.)

d) Charles and June have bought an older home and are restoring it before they move in. After they get off work in the evening, they go directly to the house where they work for several hours. One evening, Charles was refinishing the doors and ran out of sandpaper. While he went to the store to get more, June went out to buy them some sandwiches. Upon her return to the house, she noticed the front door was ajar but Charles had not returned. As she entered the house, she discovered that someone had been there while they were gone. The intruder had knocked over a bucket of nails and stolen their power sander as well as several other tools they were using in the house. Charles and June had not been gone for more than fifteen minutes. June wondered if someone was watching them. She had mixed feelings of anger and fear, and a sense of being violated. Who had done this to them? Why? Would they be returning?

e) Nancy was released after serving three years in prison. She has a daughter, Kayla, five years old, who has been in a foster home. She saw Kayla only briefly several times when the foster mother brought her to visit Nancy in prison. While in prison, Nancy got her GED and has had the opportunity to learn how to use some basic office equipment. However, she really has no job skills and no family that can provide support for her upon release. She wants to get a job, find an apartment, and, in three to six months, regain custody of Kayla. But in the meantime she needs to get a job and find a place to live. She will have $100 when she is released. She's wondering how she's going to make it. She can't go back to her old community and friends.

Where can she go?

Questions for Discussion

1. What were your feelings and reactions as you watched the dramatization and placed yourself in the story?

2. What do each of these stories say about restorative justice?

　　a. Who was harmed?

　　b. What are their needs?

　　c. Whose obligation are they?

3. What role can restorative justice play when there is a long-standing conflict which has not yet been resolved?

4. When victim and victimizer are not on equal ground, as in cases of domestic violence or in long-standing political conflicts that have not been resolved, what is the role of restorative justice?

For Additional Thought

"As we watched the towers of the World Trade Center crumble (and the Pentagon) on September 11, 2001, the shock and sense of powerlessness was overwhelming. But powerlessness is what we feel when we think we are alone and it all rests on our shoulders. The future of our world rests on all our shoulders together as we try to respond to God's calling to us for peace and justice in the world. We have a long history of overcoming powerlessness by working together, and by creating programs that give the powerless hope and ease the burden of the oppressed. A few years ago, we studied Islam and are now better equipped to advocate for tolerance rather than violence based on racial profiling" (see *Restorative Justice: Moving Beyond Punishment*, Preface).

As you read about the atrocities committed against so many totally innocent people, think about the following statement: "Without memory, there is no healing. Without forgiveness, there is no future." It is the thought-provoking comment of Peter Storey, past president of the Methodist Church of South Africa and member of the selection committee for the South Africa Truth and Reconciliation Committee (see *Restorative Justice: Moving Beyond Punishment*, ch. 4). As you think about last year's attack on the World Trade Center and the Pentagon, how do you respond to Peter Storey's statement? Does restorative justice have the same meaning for you?

Moving into the Circle of Restorative Justice

In Chapter 5 the author talks about ways of getting involved in restorative justice. He says that restorative justice is not a program, but a perspective; a set of values; an approach to doing justice; a way of life. He presents a number of hypothetical scenarios for individuals, churches, and communities.

Once more, divide into small groups and assign each group one of the stories from Chapter 5. Or you may want to give each group the opportunity of choosing from the stories listed below, selected from that chapter. Ask them to read the scenario they have chosen and respond to the questions and issues it raises. Do their responses differ when they think within the perspective of restorative justice? Allow ten to fifteen minutes for discussion and preparation. Then ask each small group to bring to the whole group a brief synopsis of the scenario and group members' responses.

1. Your child is arrested on a drug charge.

2. Should you keep a gun in your home?

3. Your daughter faces a long prison term.

4. A mosque in your town is fire-bombed.

5. Your church is faced with a murder.

6. Should this pastor break the law?

Reflecting on Personal Inventory

Ask group members to review the personal inventory sheet they filled out during the first session.

1. Have they gained new insights?

2. Have some of their previous concepts been confirmed?

3. Have some new questions been raised?

Ask them to look at the lists they began in Session 2. Do they have anything to add? Remind them that in the final session they will be examining ways of responding to these issues.

Taking It Home: Resources

Some members of the group might be leading this study for their local group. It is important for them to have resources and to know which you used and where to get them. They may have questions about what you did. This is a good time to share with them the titles of books you found helpful, particularly those on the list of the United Methodist Women reading program.

Assignments

Reading for Session 4: Chapter 6

Remind those who are to present the stories on "Making a Difference," to be prepared for the next session.

Prepare for the closing service of commitment.

H A N D O U T   3 A

Scripture: Matthew 5:43-48

Litany: Welcome, Travelers

Welcome.

   Sometimes it is harder to cross an unrepaired sidewalk than to travel a thousand miles.
   Sometimes it is harder to forgive an old friend than to welcome a stranger.
   But God teaches us that we should welcome the stranger as we would welcome Jesus
   Christ. However far we have come this week, we bring the gifts of our selves, our
   minds, our compassion, our love, and our dedication. Let us continue our journey
   together (Duck, Ruth C., ed. *Bread for the Journey*, Wheadon United Methodist Church,
      Evanston, IL, p. 27.).

Hymn: "Where Cross the Crowded Ways of Life," *The United Methodist Hymnal*, No. 427

Questions for "Listening in Order to Respond"

1. What were your feelings and responses as you watched each dramatization and placed yourself in the story?

2. What do each of these stories say about restorative justice?

     a. Who was harmed?

     d. What are their needs?

     e. Whose obligation are they?

3. What role can be played by restorative justice when there is a long-standing conflict that has not yet been resolved?

4. What is the role of restorative justice when victim and victimizer are not on equal ground, such as in cases of domestic violence or in long-standing unresolved political conflicts?

4

READING FOR THIS SESSION

Chapter 6

Goal

To look at ways in which others are working toward restorative justice in their communities as well as globally. Where do we go from here with our personal commitment?

Preparation

Handouts 4A and 4B; 3" x 5" colored cards, newsprint, markers, *The United Methodist Hymnal*, *Global Praise 1*, Bibles, copies of the closing service of commitment

Meditation

Hymn: "The Right Hand of God," *Global Praise 1*, **No. 60**

Prayer in Unison: "The Prayer of Saint Francis," *The United Methodist Hymnal*, **No. 481**

WHAT DOES IT MEAN FOR US?

In the spirit of Jesus' prophetic engagement with the dominant powers of his time, what will it take to transform the present retributive, punitive U.S. system of criminal justice into a collaborative, restorative system that encourages truth-telling, dialogue, repentance, accountability, and healing? And what will it take for us to take seriously a community's responsibility to address the root causes of crime?

As you think about the paragraph above, how do you respond to what you have learned during the course of this study about current trends in criminal justice?

1. Are there areas that you see as retributive, but are uneasy about changing?

2. Do you see them as compatible with Jesus' life and teaching? How do we turn them from retributive into restorative?

3. The author raises the issue of state-paid prison chaplains vs. those funded by the church. What is your response to the role

of the church in this matter, and how should we respond to the matter of prison chaplains?

Making a Difference

Much of this study has dealt with failing systems. However, individuals and groups are working to make a difference. There may be people in your study group who are already involved in outreach programs of restorative justice. You might ask them to tell the group about the things they are doing. (It would be good to ask them well before this meeting, so they will have time to think about it. Give them a time limit.) Following are stories of ways in which individuals and groups are working toward restorative justice. These are stories of response. Ask group members to tell these stories as examples of ways in which folks are making a difference. Present selected stories, some of which were assigned in the first session.

Refer to the lists you have been making during these study sessions. As you listen to the following stories, reflect on how they speak to the issues raised throughout the study, and on ways in which we can be involved. (See stories in *Restorative Justice: Moving Beyond Punishment,* ch.3 and shaded boxes throughout text.)

- Prison PATCH & MATCH

- Peer counseling at the McCurdy School, New Mexico

- Volunteers who provide transportation for visits to prison by the children of inmates

- Volunteer who has worked primarily with women in prison for approximately twenty years

- Church repairs done by inmates

- Articles from *Response* (May 2002) and *New World Outlook* (March-April 2002).

Working for Change

Ask the group to look back at the lists concerning restorative justice that they have been compiling throughout this study.

1. How do the above stories address them?

2. How would they set priorities in addressing needs? What issues—perhaps not listed here—do we need to work on with ongoing responses or new initiatives?

3. What are the needs in your community? What is being done to address these needs? What could be done? Begin a list of responses, or add to one that already exists. It may be wise to continue or expand something already being done. Or it might be useful to move into a new area. Some areas in which one might participate as part of a community or as an individual are shelters for victims of abuse, literacy tutoring for adults, mentoring programs for children, work with at-risk children through community centers, or assisting with the teaching of job skills.

Ask participants to divide into small groups. They may want to form the groups around certain issues or, perhaps, their home communities. They may choose to continue working in the same small group as they begin to look for ways in which they can respond to problems using the principles of restorative justice. Refer them to Handout 4A in order to respond to the questions asked throughout this study as well as to begin developing a plan for a response:

- Who is being harmed?

- What are the needs?

- Whose obligation are they?

- What can I (we) do to make a difference?

Allow time at the end for each group to present its plans.

Closing Service of Commitment

In preparation for the closing worship, distribute 3" x 5" cards. Ask participants to write how they plan to respond to the issue of restorative justice. Remind them that, while it is important that we come to learn and reflect about restorative justice, if we go home, talk about how interesting it was, and do nothing, the study has failed. There are numerous choices: leading this study in their local church; working in a mentoring program for children; volunteering at a local abuse shelter or in a local or nearby prison; continuing to work in areas in which they are already involved; and many other possibilities

Take five minutes to reflect on the following:

- What are the issues and needs?

- How are some of them currently being addressed?

- Where and how do I fit in?

- What is my commitment toward justice for others?

Ask participants to write their commitment on the card, and ask them to keep it as a reminder. At this point begin the closing service of worship and commitment. You may use the service outlined on Handout 4B, or another, prepared by one of the small groups.

H A N D O U T   4 A

Meditation

Hymn: "The Right Hand of God," *Global Praise 1*, **No. 60**

Prayer in Unison: "The Prayer of Saint Francis," *The United Methodist Hymnal*, **No. 481**

Making a Difference

Begin to examine how you as an individual or as a group may respond to the doing of restorative justice. Refer to the questions asked throughout the course of this study:

- Who is being harmed?

- What are the needs?

- Whose obligation are they?

- What can I (we) do to make a difference?

Plan for Response

1. What are you going to do? Is this something new or a continuation of what you are already doing?

2. What resources will you need? Where do you plug in?

3. Timeline

Service of Commitment

Prayer: In response to your love for us, Gracious God, we are learning to love our neighbors. It is hard to turn the other cheek when we are attacked, or to go the second mile when others place unjust demands on us. You tell us to make friends of our enemies and pray for those who seek to do us harm. We will listen to your Word, but not without protest. Engage us here in searching ourselves and wrestling with your instructions. In Jesus' name. Amen. (Lavon Bayler, *Fresh Winds of the Spirit*, New York: The Pilgrim Press, 1986, p. 34.)

Hymn: "Cuando El Pobre" (When the Poor Ones), *The United Methodist Hymnal*, No. 434

Scripture: Isaiah 58:6-12, Ephesians 2:14-18

Ask participants to take out their commitment cards and read them once more. Ask them to pray silently and reflect on how they will implement or continue their commitment. Instruct them to put their cards in a place where they will see them frequently as reminders: for example, in their Bible or wallet, or on the refrigerator.

Hymn: "Help Us Accept Each Other," *The United Methodist Hymnal*, No. 560

Sending Forth: God has shown us what is good. What does the Lord require of us but to do justice, and to love kindness, and to walk humbly with our God? Let us go out in a spirit of peace, to be prophets and liberators to those we meet. Let us commit ourselves to be instruments of justice in all that we do. Amen.

SUGGESTED OUTLINES FOR STUDIES OF ONE, TWO, OR FOUR HOURS

	ONE-HOUR STUDY	TWO-HOUR STUDY	FOUR-HOUR STUDY
SESSION ONE	Meditation As We Begin Bible Study Continuum	Meditation As We Begin Bible Study Continuum	Personal Reflection Meditation As We Begin Bible Study Continuum Restorative Justice Scenario
SESSION TWO		Video	Video Getting Down to Basics Skit: *Calling to Go*
SESSION THREE		Setting the Stage Listening to Respond	Setting the Stage Listening to Respond Reflection on Personal Inventory
SESSION FOUR	Making a Difference	Making a Difference Closing Service of Commitment	Making a Difference Second Part of Working for Change Closing Service of Commitment

B I B L I O G R A P H Y
S T U D Y   G U I D E

Coleman, John W. Jr. *Breaking Walls, Building Bridges: Confronting Violence in the United States through Mission Outreach*, General Board of Global Ministries, The United Methodist Church.

Hadjor, Kofi Buenor. *Another America: The Politics of Race and Blame*. Boston: South End Press, 1997.

Hudson, Michael. *Merchants of Misery: How Corporate America Profits from Poverty.* Monroe, ME: Common Courage Press, 1996.

Kozol, Jonathan. *Amazing Grace*. New York: Harper Perennial, 1995.

Leaver, Wayne. *Clergy and Victims of Violent Crimes Preparing for Crisis Counseling*, Lima, OH: C.S.S. Publications, Inc., 1990.

Miller, Melissa A. *Family Violence: The Compassionate Church Responds*. Scottdale, PA: Herald Press, 1994.

Perske, Robert. *Deadly Innocence?* Nashville: Abingdon Press, 1995.

Additional Material: "Within These Walls". Movie made for television, 2001 (audio-visual).

A P P E N D I X E S

PERCEPTIONS OF JUSTICE

Retributive Lens

Blame-fixing is central.

Focus is on past.

Needs are secondary.

Adversarial relationships are the norm.

Emphasis is on differences.

Imposition of pain is considered the norm.

One social injury is added to another.

Harm *by* offender is balanced by harm *to* offender.

Focus is on offender; the victim is ignored.

State and offender are the key elements.

Victims lack information.

Restitution is rare.

Victims' "truth" is secondary.

Victims' suffering is often ignored.

Action is from state to offender, whose role is passive.

State has monopoly on response to wrongdoing.

Offender has no responsibility for resolution.

Offender irresponsibility is encouraged.

Rituals of denunciation and exclusion prevail.

Offender is denounced.

Offender's ties to the community are weakened.

Fragmented view of offender is the rule.

Sense of balance is sought through retribution.

Balance is restored by lowering offender.

Justice is tested by its intent and process.

Justice is defined by the right rules.

Victim-offender relationships are ignored.

The process is alienating.

Response is based on offender's past behavior.

Restorative Lens

Problem-solving is central.

Focus is on future.

Needs are primary.

Dialogue is the norm.

There is a search for commonalities.

Restoration and repair are the norm.

Emphasis is on repair of social injuries.

Harm to offender balanced by "making it right."

Victim's needs are central.

Victim and offender are the key elements.

Information is provided to victims.

Restitution is normal.

Victims are given opportunity to tell "their truth."

Victims' suffering is acknowledged and lamented.

Offender is given role in "solution."

Victim, offender, and community have roles to play.

Offender has responsibility in resolution.

Responsible behavior is encouraged.

Rituals of lament and reordering prevail.

Harmful act is denounced.

Offender's integration into the community is increased.

Offender is viewed holistically.

Sense of balance is sought through restitution.

Balance is restored by raising both victim and and offender.

Justice is tested by its fruits.

Justice is defined by right relationships.

Victim-offender relationships are central.

The process aims at reconciliation.

Response is based on consequences of behavior.

Repentance and forgiveness are discouraged.	Repentance and forgiveness are encouraged.
Proxy professionals are the key actors.	Victim and offender are key actors, with professional help.
Competitive, individualistic values are encouraged.	Mutuality and cooperation are encouraged.
The social, economic, and moral context is ignored.	The total context is relevant.
Win-lose outcomes are assumed.	Win-win outcomes are made possible.

(Adapted from Howard Zehr, . *Changing Lenses: A New Focus for Crime and Justice.* Scottdale, PA: Herald Press, 1990.)

RESTORATIVE JUSTICE:
WHAT DOES THE LORD REQUIRE FOR THE HEALING OF THE NATIONS?

Prepared by Peggy Hutchison and excerpted from a General Board of Global Ministries resource packet distributed to GBGM directors at the annual board meeting, October 2001; the United Methodist Council of Bishops at the 2001 fall meeting; and to other GBGM constituents. Material on pp. 58-64 is excerpted from a Framework for Prayer, Discussion, and Action developed by David Wildman, executive secretary for Human Rights and Racial Justice, GBGM.

We ask God to give us strength and to guide us in the way of our United Methodist heritage which calls us to see a tragedy like what has just happened as an opportunity for self-examination, repentance, truth telling, restitution, healing, and forgiveness.

—*General Board of Global Ministries,*
September 11, 2001

Each year, as is the tradition on All Saints' Day, Christians throughout the world enter into a period of reflection and prayer to remember family, friends, and all of God's people who passed away during the previous year. For those in the United States and around the globe whose memories of September 11, 2001, were still fresh, November 1 again ushered forth the shock, horror, pain, sadness, and anger felt by so many when they learned that nineteen hijackers used three commercial airplanes to strike the World Trade Center towers and the Pentagon, and a fourth which crashed in Pennsylvania without reaching its target.

In many ways, the world seemed to spin much faster after that fateful day. Noting that life in the United States would never be the same, the nation's leaders moved to respond to this "new terrorist threat." On September 12, the United Nations Security Council adopted Resolution 1368, in which the council "expresses its readiness to take all necessary steps to respond to the terrorist attacks of 11 September 2001, and to combat all forms of terrorism, in accordance with its responsibilities under the Charter of the United Nations." On September 14, the United States Congress adopted a joint resolution (with one dissenting vote): "That the president is authorized to use all necessary and appropriate force against those nations, organizations, or persons he determines planned, authorized, committed, or aided the terrorist attacks that occurred on September 11, 2001, or harbored such organizations or persons, in order to prevent any future acts of international terrorism against the United States by such nations, organizations, or persons." On October 7, Worldwide Communion Sunday, the United States and Great Britain launched a series of massive cruise missile and bombing strikes in Afghanistan. By the end of October the news was shocking. U.S. troops had begun military operations on the ground in Afghanistan; Afghan children and other innocent civilians had been killed by U.S. cluster bombs wrapped in yellow paper (the same color as the few small plastic boxes of food also dropped from U.S. airplanes flying over Afghanistan); and misguided U.S. bombs had destroyed Red Cross warehouses and several neighborhoods and villages, killing innocent civilians. The humanitarian situation of 5 million Afghans, already desperate before September 11, had become even more precarious. Now, an additional estimated 2.5 million Afghans face the bleak reality of a severe Afghan winter with no food, little or no shelter, and no means to obtain them. In the United States, meanwhile, bioterrorism in the form of anthrax was either killing, causing illness, or scaring people throughout the land; there were increases in discrimination and hate crimes, especially against Arabs, Muslims, Asians, immigrants, and people of color; and the passage of new anti-terrorism legislation that many feared would greatly restrict human rights and due process in the United States. Each new day brought new tragedies, new fears, new horrors.

United Methodist, Methodist, and ecumenical women around the world sent letters expressing condolence, and messages of love, support, and prayer. The messages were powerful, since they came from women who have lived the daily experience of terror and violence over and over and over again. Many United Methodists around the world joined people of all faiths in seeking a restorative justice framework for prayer, discussion, and action in the aftermath of the unfolding developments in this tragic story. Joyce Sohl, deputy general secretary of the Women's Division, reflected on the challenge to United Methodist Women: "As we watched the towers of the World Trade Center crumble, the shock and sense of powerlessness was overwhelming. But powerlessness is what we feel when we think we are alone and it all rests on our shoulders. The future of our world rests on all our shoulders together as we try to respond to God's calling to us for peace and justice in the world. We have a long history of overcoming powerlessness by working together, and by creating programs that give the powerless hope and ease the burden of the oppressed. This spirit is calling us to come together. United Methodist Women are needed more than ever to come together through prayer, action, and financial support."

The struggle to sow seeds of restorative justice around the world, especially in times of war, has taught God's people that there is no one answer nor a quick fix. The following questions provide such a framework for our reflection.

I. Why Did This Happen?: Examining the Root Causes of Terror and Violence

The Psalmist cries out repeatedly, Why O Lord? (e.g., Psalms 2, 10; Habakkuk 1). Painful as it may be, part of the call to love our enemies includes trying to discern the reasons for their actions. Little children, in their persistence, remind us that asking why is a long-term process. Children are not satisfied with one explanation, but keep asking why? How can each of us stand in the shoes of our enemies, our neighbors, those we disagree with, and try and understand another's pain even as we condemn violent actions? What would motivate persons to engage in such violent attacks, taking their own lives? From the perspective of Afghan refugees, from the perspective of Muslims, why are the United States and Britain bombing a poor Muslim country? What things in U.S. foreign policy might have caused a degree of pain and suffering that would spark such deep resentment in others? Why have yesterday's "freedom fighters" (Osama bin Laden and the Taliban) become today's "terrorists"? Why do nations in the West continue to support violent, corrupt, undemocratic regimes that repress their own people (e.g., Saudi Arabia)? Why is violence of the weak "terrorism," while violence of the powerful is "self-defense"? Finally, will we of the church encourage our members and our leaders to avoid simplistic answers, and keep asking why?

II. Reflections on War and Peace

Christians have historically expressed a variety of stands on war and violence, ranging from pacifism to reluctant endorsement of "just" wars, to militant crusades against evil enemies. The Social Principles (165C) state, "We believe war is incompatible with the teachings and example of Christ. We therefore reject war as a usual instrument of national foreign policy." The resolution "Consequences of Conflict" sets forth criteria for all who "choose to take up arms or who order others to do so to evaluate their actions in accordance with historic church teaching limiting resort to war." The just-war theory frequently serves as a means for governments to justify their military actions and has rarely, if ever, served to stop military action before it starts. However, the criteria put forth as the basis for a just war help us raise key questions about military action as a just or effective means of ending a situation of extreme violence and injustice. In the just-war tradition, all seven criteria must be fully addressed in order to consider resorting to military action in

pursuit of justice. In the process of addressing each of these, many alternatives to force will be examined.

A. *Just Cause.* This criterion addresses root causes of violent acts and appropriate level of remedy. Such discussion of causes and remedies deserves full public consideration of why violence and acts of war or terror took place. Examining root causes provides an opportunity for each nation to examine the "log in our own eye" in terms of foreign policy, immigration policy, and Christian attitudes, especially toward the Middle East and Islamic communities. The world community has expressed remarkable unity in condemnation and in calls to bring those responsible to justice. What remedies conform with the norms of international law and restorative justice? Difficult as it is, it is important to consider the just-cause question from the standpoint of the perpetrators, as well. While nothing can justify the violence and targeting of noncombatants on September 11, what factors may have motivated some to engage in such violent acts? As we noted earlier, analysts have observed in the past that one person's terrorist is another's freedom fighter, and vice versa. In establishing just cause specifically for military action, how important is it to account for, debate, and respond to the arguments of one's enemies?

B. *Just Intent.* Even when a cause for military action is considered just, according to just-war theory, one must evaluate the intent of the parties that plan to wage war as a remedy. Are the intentions behind each possible type of military action and each possible target just? Or, in some cases, may other motives be driving the resort to military action?

C. *Last Resort.* Perhaps most important of the seven criteria for undertaking a just war is that military action must be a last resort. In response to horrendous violence and suffering it is understandable that many seek immediate justice, retaliation, or revenge. Yet, justifiable anger does not justify any and all actions. Short of military force, have all diplomatic, legal, and other multilateral means of bringing to justice the people responsible for the devastating attacks of September 11 been fully tried and exhausted? For instance, should charges first be brought before an international tribunal or the International Criminal Court, and should those legal avenues be fully exhausted before resorting to military force?

D. *Probability of Success.* The use of conventional forces and weapons of mass destruction against guerrilla forces or small groups has had a low probability of success in the past. Even with its powerful military, the Soviet Union had little success during ten years of military action in Afghanistan. In the so-called war against terrorism, what constitutes success? Is apprehending and/or killing any and all suspected terrorists, terrorist organizations, and any who would harbor or support such groups the measure of success? If so, how likely is it that such an end can be achieved? If military strikes generate a

new round of violent acts in response, which in turn spark further military actions, how probable is success in ending the cycle of violence? Each military strategy currently used or being considered should be evaluated in this light.

E. *Legal Authority.* Broad power to wage war was authorized by the U.S. Congress. Is this authorization sufficient under international law to permit armed forces and military strikes into other nations? What role should the UN Security Council play in authorizing any specific military action? What burden of proof is needed to justify various levels of military action against any particular nation? Many people consider the attacks of September 11 to be criminal acts because they were committed by a group of individuals and not a nation. In that case, the appropriate response might be within in the framework of international criminal law, the International Criminal Court or special international tribunal, and not that of war. Who is the appropriate legal authority to decide the nature of this act and the appropriate response? Does the UN charter's right to self-defense (Article 51) include the authority to attack and invade another country in the name of pursuing justice against suspected criminals? (For instance, the majority of the members of the UN Security Council and of the General Assembly voted to condemn the invasion of Panama in 1989 when the United States sought to apprehend Noriega. Legal charges and proceedings for extradition—not military force—have been, and are being, used against Augusto Pinochet and Ariel Sharon. UN-authorized sanctions and other forms of non-military international pressure were used against Libya to extradite two suspects for the bombing of a plane.)

F. *Proportionality.* What constitutes a proportional military response to a violent act that targets civilians? Is the use of weapons of mass destruction by the United States and others (e.g., cruise missiles, cluster bombs) proportional, given past experience (one of the cruise missiles fired against bin Laden's camp in 1998 landed hundreds of miles away in Pakistan). What criteria for proportionality do we use: number of casualties already inflicted; number of potential casualties; amount of so-called "collateral damage"? "An eye for an eye" might suggest that casualties should be limited to 6,000. [Based on casualty figures given just after the attacks on September 11, 2001.] What level of casualties would lead us to declare that the "cure" of waging war is worse than the original crime? Are refugees who die of starvation and exposure considered part of this proportional equation?

G. *Discrimination Between Combatants and Noncombatants.* In the last half of the twentieth century, roughly 90 percent of casualties in conflicts were noncombatants. The protection of noncombatants has been systematically violated in almost every conflict for the past fifty years. In the first few days of bombing, several UN de-mining personnel in Afghanistan were killed by U.S. bombs. On October 16, World Food Day, a Red Cross warehouse containing blankets, wheat, and other humanitarian provisions (and with a large cross on its roof!) was hit by two bombs from an F-18 fighter plane, destroying most of the supplies and injuring a guard. The exact number of Afghan civilian deaths and wounded is, so far, not known.

What assurances do we have that current military actions in response to September 11 will be in keeping with The United Methodist Church's resolution on terrorism that calls United Methodist Christians to "oppose the use of indiscriminate military force to combat terrorism, especially where the use of such force results in casualties among noncombatant citizens who are not themselves perpetrators of terrorist acts"? Who will monitor the protection of civilians during today's military strikes? How do we evaluate the targeting and destroying of office buildings, water- and sewage-treatment plants, power plants, pharmaceutical factories, nuclear reactors, schools, hospitals, etc., in terms of their impact on noncombatants? Are such methods as the use of weapons of mass destruction (cruise missiles, depleted-uranium-tipped warheads), carpet-bombing from B-52s, and the dropping of anti-personnel mines discriminating or not? Are economic sanctions and military blockades of a whole nation discriminating or not? Is a war that displaces thousands of Afghans as refugees discriminating or not?

III. Expanded Use of Covert Action

Legislation has been introduced in the U.S. Congress, and similar measures are being considered in other nations, to reduce or eliminate many current restrictions on covert actions, such as impersonating missionaries or journalists, hiring people with criminal or violent records, providing weapons to groups with known human rights violations, and even orders to carry out assassinations. In the name of fighting terrorism, terrorists, and those who harbor terrorist organizations, many governments may resort to more covert actions. As Christians, what stand should we take on the use of covert operations? What means, if any, are morally justified? Will some militant factions be supported to target other militant factions? This is part of what happened when the United States pumped $3 billion into covert operations in Afghanistan throughout the 1980s (The CIA-funded covert operation in Afghanistan was the largest such covert operation in history.)

IV. How Does the Church Support and Offer Guidance to Both Military Personnel and Those Seeking Conscientious Objection Status— Especially in the Face of War?

The Social Principles state the following: "We urge all young adults to seek the counsel of the church as they reach a conscientious decision concerning the nature of their responsibility as citizens.... We support and extend the ministry of the Church to those persons who conscientiously oppose all war, or any particular wars ...[and] we support and extend the Church's ministry to those persons who conscientiously choose to 'recognize the right of individuals to dissent.'" (Para. 164E) In what ways are churches encouraging and supporting young people to reflect on the range of options they face in wartime? Would churches consider offering sanctuary to persons who conscientiously oppose the use of military force in the war against terror or to persons currently serving in the military who in good conscience oppose the way the current war is being waged, even as they also offer support to persons serving in the military?

V. How Can the Church Combat Hate and Discrimination?

How can the church strengthen and broaden its educational and advocacy efforts in ministries that address crimes of hate and violence—ministries that enable the church to stand in solidarity with a large range of people and groups: Arabs, Muslims, Asians, immigrants, people of color, peace groups, groups engaged in political dissent, and others targeted through hateful speech and violence? The American-Arab Anti-Discrimination Committee (founded in 1980) has already documented several hundred reported incidents of hate, harassment, and violence, including three murders. How does the church address institutional discrimination, such as racial profiling by police and other security personnel, in a climate of increased fear and heightened security measures?

VI. Response to Proposed Anti-Terror Legislation and Government Policies

Many civil liberty and religious groups fear that the anti-terror legislation will greatly restrict human rights and due process, especially for immigrants. How can we insure the fullest protection of civil liberties and human rights for all of God's children, even as governments seek to expand wiretapping, search warrants, and other law enforcement powers to deal with real and perceived threats?

VII. Protecting Refugees and Other Uprooted People in Afghanistan

The humanitarian situation of Afghans was already desperate before the September 11 attacks. Now, with U.S. military strikes that, though directed against Taliban forces, have hit villages and neighborhoods, the situation of these 7.5 million people is even more precarious. Already in the first few days of the war, the cost of the U.S. bombing exceeds the annual gross domestic product of all Afghanistan. Yet, according to the UN, the international community has provided virtually no funding for humanitarian relief. By the end of October, the United States had airdropped 200,000 meal packets (each good for one person for one day). Assuming none of them were damaged, or landed in minefields, or were seized by the Taliban, they might have provided three to four percent of the refugees with one day's food. All of this, even as massive bombings destroyed two Red Cross warehouses and cut off virtually all truck deliveries of food. Is this a genuine humanitarian effort or a propaganda effort to deflect criticism? What actions can we take to insure that the safety and human rights of all uprooted peoples in and around Afghanistan are fully protected?

VIII. Military Spending Versus Social and Development Spending

While much attention is focused on military action, there is a marked shift in governmental priorities and allocation of resources toward more weapons, including Star Wars. How can the church address people's security concerns in keeping with our emphasis on peace with justice rather than militarized measures? Every dollar devoted to military spending means one dollar less for development needs. James Wolfensohn, head of the World Bank, reflecting on the global consequences following September 11, said, "There is another human toll that is largely unseen and one that will be felt in all parts of the developing world, especially Africa. We estimate that tens of thousands more children will die worldwide and some 10 million more people are likely to be living below the poverty line of $1 a day because of the terrorist attacks. This is simply from loss of income. Many, many more people will be thrown into poverty if development strategies are disrupted." How can the churches insure that resources for seeds and plowshares are not redirected into the making of swords?

IX. Congressional and Community Listening Projects

How do churches allow and encourage people with differing views to come together to discuss ways of seeking peace and restorative justice? What pastoral responsibilities do churches have to persons with dissenting views? In a time of war and heightened security measures, what would it mean for the church to offer sanctuary?

X. Interfaith Activities

How can churches, in cooperation with Muslim organizations, foster better understanding and relations with our Muslim neighbors? See resolution entitled "Our Muslim Neighbors." (The Book of Resolutions) Following the attacks of September 11, United Methodist, ecumenical, and Muslim women in Senegal joined together in worship services and prayers for peace and justice. How can existing interfaith efforts in the Democratic Republic of Congo, Sierra Leone,

Palestine, Egypt, Philippines, and Bosnia, for example, be lifted up as models for other communities and regions?

XI. Media Monitoring and Accountability

In times of conflict and war, it is even more important to monitor media coverage and to seek out a variety of perspectives. Are voices of dissent and other global perspectives being heard at local, national, and international levels? What steps can churches take to engage editors, reporters, and other media outlets to prevent stereotyping or demonizing of certain ethnic groups and/or religions?

XII. Promoting and Protecting Human Rights for All, in a Context of Fear and Violence

How can churches work to insure that human rights violations do not escalate or get overlooked in the name of fighting terrorism? Will the international community remain quiet about human rights violations and attacks against civilians in Chechnya, Colombia, Palestine, and many other places?

XIII. Relationship to Other Regional and Internal Conflicts

What connections are there—or are being made—between the war in Afghanistan and other regional and internal conflicts? For instance, what impact will the current war in Afghanistan have on the ongoing Israeli military occupation of Palestine; on sanctions and strikes against Iraq; on the conflict between India and Pakistan over Kashmir; on conflicts in Nigeria, Sudan, Democratic Republic of Congo; on possible government targeting of militant Islamic groups in other countries (e.g., in Philippines, Indonesia, Algeria, Egypt)? How does the church work to strengthen international cooperation in pursuit of conflict resolution, justice, and peace and development rather than violence in each of these contexts?

THE BOOK OF RESOLUTIONS OF
THE UNITED METHODIST CHURCH, 2000:
SOCIAL PRINCIPLES (PARA. 164, V, F)

Criminal and Restorative Justice—To protect all persons from encroachment upon their personal and property rights, governments have established mechanisms of law enforcement and courts. A wide array of sentencing options serves to express community outrage, incapacitate dangerous offenders, deter crime, and offer opportunities for rehabilitation. We support governmental measures designed to reduce and eliminate crime that are consistent with respect for the basic freedom of persons.

We reject all misuse of these mechanisms, including their use for the purpose of revenge or for persecuting or intimidating those whose race, appearance, lifestyle, economic condition, or beliefs differ from those in authority. We reject all careless, callous or discriminatory enforcement of law that withholds justice from all non-English speaking persons and persons with disabilities. We further support measures designed to remove the social conditions that lead to crime, and we encourage continued positive interaction between law enforcement officials and members of the community at large.

In the love of Christ, who came to save those who are lost and vulnerable, we urge the creation of a genuinely new system for the care and restoration of victims, offenders, criminal justice officials, and the community as a whole. Restorative justice grows out of biblical authority, which emphasizes a right relationship with God, self, and community. When such relationships are violated or broken through crime, opportunities are created to make things right.

Most criminal justice systems around the world are retributive. These retributive justice systems profess to hold the offender accountable to the state and use punishment as the equalizing tool for accountability. In contrast, restorative justice seeks to hold the offender accountable to the victimized person, and to the disrupted community. Through God's transforming power, restorative justice seeks to repair the damage, right the wrong, and bring healing to all involved, including the victim, the offender, the families, and the community. The Church is transformed when it responds to the claims of discipleship by becoming an agent of healing and systemic change.

Appendix D

THE BOOK OF RESOLUTIONS OF THE UNITED METHODIST CHURCH, 2000: RESTORATIVE JUSTICE (NO. 241)

I. Biblical Theological Grounding

The words of Micah ring out clearly, setting the tone for justice ministries in the church: "He has told you, 0 Mortal, what is good, and what does the Lord require of you but to do justice, and to love kindness, and to walk humbly with your God?" (Micah 6:8)

Justice is the basic principle upon which God's creation has been established. It is an integral and uncompromising part in God's redemptive process, which assures wholeness. Compassion is characterized by sensitivity to God's justice and, therefore, sensitivity to God's people.

The gospel, through the example of Jesus Christ, conveys the message for Christians to be healers, peacemakers, and reconcilers when faced with brokenness, violence, and vengeance. Through love, caring, and forgiveness, Jesus Christ is able to transform lives and restore dignity and purpose in those who are willing to abide by his principles.

Jesus was concerned about victims of crime. In the story of the Good Samaritan, Jesus explored the responsibility we have for those who have been victimized: "'Which of these three, do you think, was neighbor to the man who fell into the hands of the robbers?' He said, 'The one who showed him mercy.' Jesus said to him, 'Go and do likewise'" (Luke 10:36-37).

Jesus was concerned about offenders, those who victimize others. He rejected vengeance and retribution as the model of justice to be used for relating to offenders: "You have heard that it was said, 'An eye for an eye and a tooth for a tooth.' But I say to you, Do not resist an evildoer. But if anyone strikes you on the right cheek, turn the other also" (Matthew 5:38ff). Jesus also indicated the responsibility Christians have for offenders: "I was sick and you took care of me, I was in prison and you visited me. . . .Truly I tell you, just as you did it to one of the least of these . . . you did it to me" (Matthew 25:36, 40).

The Apostle Paul believed that this biblical concept of justice which was reflected in the life of Christ was a primary molder of Christian community and responsibility: "All this is from God, who reconciled us to himself through Christ, and has given us the ministry of reconciliation; that is, in Christ, God was reconciling the world to himself, not counting their trespasses against them, and entrusting the message of reconciliation to us" (2 Corinthians 5:18-19).

While acknowledging that the biblical concept of justice focuses on the victim, the offender, and the community in the hope of restoring all to a sense of God's wholeness, it is also important to understand that our Methodist heritage is rich with examples of ministries carried out in jails and prisons. John Wesley (and others in his inner circle, including a brother, Charles) had a passion for those in prison. As early as 1778, the Methodist Conference adopted action making it the duty of every Methodist preacher to minister to those who were incarcerated. United Methodists have reaffirmed and expanded the mandate for prison ministry and reform in many different chapters of our denominational history. This is a part of our identity and call.

Criminal justice in our world rarely focuses on the biblical initiatives of restoration, mercy, wholeness, and shalom. Out of a desire to punish rather than restore, governments around the world have made retribution the heart of their criminal justice systems, believing that this will deter crime and violence. The statistics indicate the colossal failure of retributive justice. Therefore, we call on the church to embrace the biblical concept of restorative justice as a hopeful alternative to our present criminal justice codes. Restorative justice focuses on the victim, the offender, and the community in the desire to bring healing and wholeness to all.

II. Our Current Criminal Justice System: A Retributive Justice System

A. *Victims:* When crime is defined as the breaking of a law, the state (rather than the victim) is posited as the primary victim. Criminal justice, as we know it, focuses little or no attention on the needs of the victim. Legal proceedings inadvertently cause crime victims, including loved ones, to experience shock and a sense of helplessness which is further exacerbated by financial loss, spiritual and emotional trauma, and often a lack of support and direction. Many victims feel frustrated because, in most cases, there seems to be little or no provision for them to be heard or to be notified of court proceedings. Victims, moreover, are seldom given the opportunity to meet with their offenders, face to face, in order to personally resolve their conflicts and to move toward healing, authentic reconciliation, and closure.

B. *Offenders:* Our criminal justice systems around the world have become based on retribution. Although it is often cloaked or justified in the language of accountability this focus on punishment has resulted in massive increases in the number of incarcerated persons across the globe. In the United States, for example, the prison population doubled between 1990 and 2000, even as the crime rate decreased during this period. Because prisons are often places where dehumanizing conditions reinforce negative behavior, present criminal justice systems actually perpetuate a cycle of violence, crime, and incarceration, especially among those whose race, appearance, lifestyle, economic conditions, or beliefs differ from those in authority.

Incarceration is costly. In the United States, the cost of incarcerating someone for a year ranges between $15,000 and $30,000. Citizens are therefore paying billions of dollars for the support of systems that consistently engender a grossly dehumanizing experience characterized by the loss of freedom, the loss of contact with family and friends, the loss of self-determination, the loss of education, the loss of adequate medical care, and the loss of religious freedom and opportunities for spiritual growth.

C. *Community:* Criminal justice, as we know it, is retributive justice. It is consumed with blame and pain. It is a system of retribution that pays little or no consideration to the root causes of criminal behavior. It does not aim at solutions that will benefit the whole community by helping the community to repair the breach and often fails to come to terms with the social conditions that breed crime. Retributive justice permanently stigmatizes the offender for past actions, thereby creating such a sense of alienation from the community that social reintegration is virtually impossible. An offender who is held in exile away from the community cannot be held accountable to the community for his or her wrongdoing. An ex-offender who is ostracized and kept in exile after paying his or her debt to society is further violated. He or she is stripped of the opportunity to fully understand the consequences of the crime committed, to make restitution to the victim, to be reconciled with the community or to heal and become a viable member of the community.

III. Our Vision Of Restorative Justice

The gospel, through the example of Jesus Christ, conveys the message for Christians to be healers, peacemakers, and reconcilers when faced with brokenness, violence, and vengeance. The concept of restorative justice shows us specific ways by which to transform lives and effect healing.

Restorative justice asks: Who has been hurt? What are their needs? Whose obligations are they?

We label the person who has been hurt "the victim." But the victim is essentially a survivor who need not remain a victim for his or her entire life.

The victim needs healing and emotional support. Victims (survivors) want people to recognize the trauma they have endured and how this trauma has affected their lives and the lives of their loved ones. Often survivors/victims need counseling, assistance, compensation, information, and services. Victims/survivors need to participate in their own healing. They may need reparations from the offender, or the victim may want to meet the offender and have input during the trial, sentencing, and rehabilitation process.

During the healing process, the victim often asks: Why me? What kind of person could do such a thing? Therefore, they may want to meet their offender to receive answers to such questions. Victims deserve to have these questions answered and to hear that the offender is truly sorry.

Victims suffer real pain; however, encouraging vengeance does not heal pain. The community needs to aid in the recovery of the victim. The community and can help by not ostracizing him or her, by learning how to accept him or her as a person and not just a victim.

Offenders are harmed as well. An offender is harmed by being labeled for life as an offender. One or more bad decisions or actions sometimes measure the total of an offender's life. Offenders are harmed further when they are denied the opportunity to make amends, to have respectful interaction with others, and to develop healthy social skills before, during, or after incarceration. Often young offenders do not have constructive guidance or a good role model in the community. Sometimes they need treatment for a disorder, life skills development, or mentoring with clear and achievable expectations of heightened self-awareness and accountability.

The victim and the community need to identify ways the offender can remedy hurt and harm caused. The offender needs to understand how his or her behavior affected others, and acknowledge that the behavior was indeed harmful. The offender needs to be transformed into a contributing citizen of the community with a system of limits and support.

Crime hurts the community. When crime occurs, the neighborhood is disrupted; people become more isolated, fearful, distrusting, and uninterested in the community. Restorative justice helps to release the community members from their fear of crime; it empowers them with the knowledge that circumstances are not out of their control. The community needs to express pain and anger to the one or ones who caused the harm. However, we need to take one step further by helping in the healing process. We need to understand and address the causes of crime to prevent future occurrences. The victim, community and offender (when possible) need to help others who face similar struggles.

Restorative justice opens the opportunities for personal and community transformation. This transformation cannot be mapped, planned, or put into a program or structure. Nevertheless, it can be encouraged and nurtured.

United Methodists have the will, the vision, the opportunity and the responsibility to be advocates for systemic change. We are called to minister with all parties affected by crime: the victim, the offender and the community.

Expectations are high for the faith community to lead the way in practicing restorative justice. We need to own and advocate a vision of restorative justice. We need to be supportive to members of the congregation who are victims, offenders, and their families, and especially to those who work toward restoration in the criminal justice system.

The church must initiate models of restorative justice with service providers, policy makers, and law enforcement. We need to work in partnership with the criminal justice system to make it more open, accessible, humane, effective, and rehabilitative, and less costly. We need to see our own complicity in community breakdowns and in the racism and classism present in the enactment and enforcement of criminal law. We must also advocate for social and economic justice to see the restoration and strengthening of our communities.

IV. A Call To Action

As United Methodists we are called to:

- repent of the sin we have committed that has fostered retributive justice;

- speak prophetically and consistently against dehumanization in the criminal justice system;

- establish restorative justice as the theological ground for ministries in The United Methodist Church and to build bridges of collaboration and cooperation to advance the practice of restorative justice with boards and agencies within The United Methodist Church, with United Methodist and other Methodist communions around the globe, with other faith communities in the United States and worldwide; and with nonprofit organizations, and/or governmental organizations;

- intensify our redemptive ministries with those who work in criminal justice, victims of crime and their families, those who are incarcerated in jails and prisons and their families, and communities traumatized by crime.

At the General Church Level:

1 Restorative Justice Ministries Inter-Agency Task Force:

Continue and expand the work of The United Methodist Church's Restorative Justice Ministries through the Inter-Agency Task Force, which serves as the global coordinating committee for criminal justice and mercy ministries mandated by the 1996 General Conference of The United Methodist Church, by the following:

Maintain and broaden the involvement of general agencies in this task force, including: the General Board of Global Ministries (as "lead" or "administrative agency"), the General Board of Discipleship, the General Board of Higher Education and Ministry, the General Board of Church and Society, the General Council on Ministries, the Council of Bishops, and other relevant agencies and initiatives.

Fulfill these specific functions:

provide a biblical-theological basis for a restorative justice approach to criminal justice;

be a center for resourcing, teaching, learning, and networking;

work collegially with other groups and organizations whether they are inside or outside the denomination, religious or secular, by finding common ground to bring about systemic change in the spirit of mediation (even when there is disagreement about theological rationale); coordinate the training, networking, and advocacy for Restorative

Justice Ministries of The United Methodist Church by working with jurisdictions, annual conferences, central conferences, districts, local United Methodist churches and their communities.

serve as the primary advocate and interpreter of Restorative Justice Ministries;

identify and expand critical models and facilitate the development of Restorative Justice Ministries, on a global basis, at all levels of The United Methodist Church. Manage the Restorative Justice Ministries budget and assist in procuring additional funding for these ministries in strategic locations across the church.

2 Specific General Church Agencies:

A. *Identify and implement disciplinary functions that can strengthen The United Methodist Church's effectiveness in the area of restorative justice.*

B. *Continue to implement and expand the special mandates from the 1996 General Conference.*

■ that United Methodist Women consider the integration of Restorative Justice Ministries within the Schools of Christian Ministry as they develop study curricula;

■ that the General Board of Global Ministries consider naming missionaries in the fields of prison ministry and victims' advocacy ministry;

■ that central conferences and annual conferences in the United States be linked through electronic mail, when available, so that frequent communication can enhance the planning process for this new initiative;

- that the General Board of Discipleship be responsible for the training of local church and annual conference leaders to utilize study processes such as Disciple Bible Study and/or Covenant Discipleship, and to provide mentoring;

- that United Methodist Men and United Methodist Women give consideration to starting units within jails and prisons and create study guides and tools to promote Christian disciple-making;

- that existing programs and resources be evaluated to assess their applicability and effectiveness in ministries with victims, families, and those incarcerated;

- that the General Board of Higher Education and Ministry and the General Board of Discipleship consider the development of a certification process for those providing ministries with prisoners, crime victims, and their families;

- that the General Board of Church and Society and the General Board of Global Ministries intensify their advocacy for social and economic justice in order to restore and strengthen communities;

- that the General Board of Church and Society and the General Board of Global Ministries continue to advocate for a criminal justice system that is not racist, less costly, and more humane, effective, rehabilitative, and accessible to family members of victims and offenders.

At Jurisdictional Central Conference and Annual Conference Levels:

1 Support jurisdictional/central conference and annual conference networking as modeled by the Southeastern jurisdiction's Criminal Justice and Mercy Ministries network, or bring together clusters of contiguous conferences or expedite processes of training and resource sharing.

2 Encourage conferences to establish interagency restorative justice task forces to coordinate Restorative Justice Ministries within their bounds, with special emphasis on partnership with the Restorative Justice Ministries Interagency Task Force and the facilitation and resourcing of local church ministries.

At the Local Level:

1 Encourage local congregations to provide adult and youth education programs on restorative justice: theory practice, issues, models, resources (utilizing curriculum resources, printed and audiovisual, provided through the above mentioned connectional sources).

2 Encourage congregations to provide safe space to enable people to share real experiences of victimization, incarceration, or other direct encounters with the criminal justice system and/or restorative justice processes.

3 Encourage congregations to schedule a "Restorative Justice Ministries Sunday" to generate deeper awareness by the entire congregation regarding the contrasting paradigms of retributive justice and restorative justice and their different outcomes.

4 Encourage congregations to organize or form direct service and/or advocacy efforts to support the work of restorative justice.

5 Work with local ecumenical and/or interfaith agencies and other community agencies to:

- Convene consultations of representatives of the restorative justice community to define policy/legislative needs and strategies.

- Encourage/resource congregations to work on restorative justice—working through regional judicatories and media.

- Encourage/initiate dialogue with correctional/criminal justice system officials.

- Identify and nurture criminal justice system leaders (e.g., judges, attorneys, wardens, police, etc.) regarding restorative justice.

- Involve local congregations in ministries with juvenile detention centers and domestic violence centers.

- Build covenant discipleship groups at the local level for restorative justice advocates, as well as for other persons involved in the criminal justice system.

- Promote victim-offender mediation and other restorative justice processes.

- Identify and develop coalitional partnerships with victim assistance groups, advocacy groups, jail and prison ministry groups, ex-offender assistance groups, etc.

- Plan and implement strategies, for advocacy that encourage legislative support for restorative justice programs.

ADOPTED 2000
From *The Book of Resolutions*
of The United Methodist Church – 2000
Copyright © 2000
by The United Methodist Publishing House
Used by permission. October 31, 2001

THE DEATH PENALTY

by Harmon L. Wray

Juries

Lawyers' jargon for jury selection in a capital murder case is "death qualification": picking a jury qualified to judge the defendant's guilt or innocence, as well as determine punishment. Prosecutor and defense counsel look for jurors who are likely to lean toward their side. Each is granted a certain number of "strikes"—removing potential jurors either without stating a specific reason, or "for cause." The judge may also dismiss a potential juror. Judge and prosecutor look for potential jurors who indicate that they have no problem considering the death penalty for a defendant found guilty.

This means that the defendant's assumed right to a jury of peers is constrained by the fact that, unless they perjure themselves during questioning, persons with serious scruples about the death penalty are not likely to wind up on the jury.

The accused is also at a disadvantage because "death-qualified" jurors are more likely than members of a non-capital jury to convict the defendants as well as mete out the death penalty. The main advantage for the defendant is that usually a jury verdict must be unanimous—first to find guilt, then to hand down a death sentence.

Jurors, like others in the process, are encouraged to regard themselves as simply "carrying out the law," rather than exercising personal moral responsibility for the death penalty or a life sentence. They are usually not given information about what a life sentence really means in terms of the possibility and minimum eligibility requirements for parole; what right they have to judge the validity of the death penalty law itself (the "jury nullification" principle operative in some states); how major religious traditions perceive the legitimacy of the death penalty; issues of deterrence and economic cost; and how matters of race and class affect the meting out of the death penalty. Sometimes they are not even permitted to know whether the victim's family is in favor of a death sentence.

Race, Class, and Mental Health

Americans are gradually realizing that, in the past as well as today, many more people of color than whites have received the death penalty, even though their percentages of the population are just the opposite. More than two dozen studies have consistently shown that persons accused of killing white victims are from four to ten times more likely to receive death sentences than those charged with killing blacks, in both northern and southern states. Similar patterns are reflected in the socio-economic class of victims and defendants.

Indeed, the most common characteristics of those who wind up on death row are these:

1. they are poor;

2. they are charged with killing a white middle- or upper-class person;

3. they had a bad lawyer—usually court-appointed instead of hired—who had few resources to work with;

4. they come from an abusive home and may have permanent brain damage from serious head injuries.

Money

From a taxpayer's perspective, the death penalty is surprisingly expensive. Because our Constitution's Bill of Rights includes substantial safeguards for due process, and because most people charged with capital murder are indigent, public funds must pay the very high legal costs of capital trials and appeals. They must also cover the expense of extra security for pretrial confinement and confinement on death row, as well as the cost of the executions themselves. Studies in California, New York, Texas, Indiana, Kansas, Florida, Michigan, New Jersey, and North Carolina show that governments spend several times more in taxpayers' money for capital cases (especially trials), death row custody, and executions than would be the cost of life sentences for all first-degree murderers.

Deterrence and Victims

Some death penalty proponents insist that the cost of these executions is money well spent (or would be if we carried out more of them) because of the benefits to society. Until recently, the claim that executions deter others from committing murder ("general deterrence") was the primary argument for capital punishment, but numerous studies failed to demonstrate that this is so. Some have even suggested that executions may increase the number of murders. The reason, they maintain, is social "brutalization" resulting from legally sanctioned violence, or through murders committed by unstable persons because of a death wish or a hunger for the notoriety that an execution often brings. In any case, the real issue is whether or not capital punishment has any discernible deterrent effect greater than that of other available sentences, i.e., lengthy or permanent life imprisonment. Common sense and the empirical evidence indicate that it does not.

In recent years, death penalty advocates stressed two other rationales for executions: that those who are executed will commit no more murders ("specific deterrence"); and that executions clearly express society's moral outrage over unlawful killing and, on behalf of the whole society, provide an appropriate and satisfying sense of retribution for the families and friends of murder victims.

In response to the "specific deterrence" rationale for the death penalty, those who advocate abolishing capital punishment contend that either life without parole or a mandatory sentence of twenty-five years (or longer) before eligibility for parole takes murderers as completely out of commission as do executions—and without the risk of executing innocent people. The issue of innocence has become an important public concern, especially since a study in the 1990s demonstrated that in the United States, during the twentieth century, at least twenty-three innocent persons were executed.

In answer to society's proper moral outrage,

abolitionists argue that a murder conviction followed by long years of serving a life (or lengthy) prison sentence sends a stronger message about the unacceptability of killing than when society kills the killers. They also suggest that the death penalty tends to further victimize the families of murder victims by focusing public attention on the killer instead of the victim, and by drawing out the judicial ritual (and, thus, the cycle of grief) for many years. Capital punishment, say death penalty opponents, denies the surviving family what it needs and could achieve: significant, though partial, restitution or other financial compensation for their massive loss; the possibility of genuine repentance by the murderer; a quicker resolution of the grief process so that families can go on with their lives. Abolitionists also say that capital punishment, unable to restore the murder victim, worsens the overall situation by creating more victims—the family of the executed offender.

Public Opinion and Alternatives

If the death penalty is so unacceptable, what exists that would be better and has a chance of being enacted? The good news is that the signals are clear, if our politicians and other leaders can muster the political will and moral courage to act on them. A series of sophisticated public opinion surveys has been developed and carried out in a number of states, as well as nationally. These studies go beyond the usual "Are you for or against the death penalty?" and "Why are you for it?" questions that characterize most public opinion polls concerning this issue. Such polls inevitably show the American public as overwhelmingly in favor of capital punishment. Many give retribution or revenge as their primary reason for supporting

the ultimate sanction, but others say that specific deterrence is more important. Thus, the results are mixed.

When no alternative to capital punishment is specified, the more sophisticated polls yield similar results on the "for/against" scale. But when respondents are asked about the specific alternative of life without parole (LWOP) for murder convictions, they tend to prefer that option to the death penalty, or, at least, to show roughly equal numbers for the two options.

When surveyors go one step further, however, and ask respondents to choose between death and a sentence of LWOP coupled with a requirement to work in prison industries and pay financial restitution to the murder victim's family, the responses change. In California, Florida, and New York, respondents in overwhelming numbers chose LWOP and restitution over death. The attraction of restitution appears to be so great that—even when coupled with a mandatory minimum sentence of twenty-five years before parole eligibility instead of natural life (LWOP)—respondents in several death-penalty states still favor this option by substantial margins.

Enough data have been gathered from enough different places to constitute a direct and unmistakable signal from the American people: When presented with alternatives that address their goals for responding to violent crime, they prefer the non-deadly option. It is equally clear what those goals are: 1) protection of society from those who have killed, and 2) justice, with some sense of fairness, for murder victims' families. If they do not believe that they can get protection from killers in the form of lengthy imprisonment, they will choose death over what they see as the risk of early release and repeat murders. Similarly, without a meaningful option for restitution, they opt for death as payback.

It is apparent that the American public is misinformed about a number of things: 1) the length of prison sentences for first-degree murder (actually, very long in every state); 2) the number of those who become repeat killers (negligible); 3) the quality of life in prison (abysmal); 4) the degree of unfairness and inequity in the application of the death penalty (even worse than most people think); and 5) the relative economic costs of death versus life imprisonment. In recent years, however, issues of fairness and of judicial mistakes have risen to the fore. Illinois has declared a moratorium on executions, and a number of other states are studying the death penalty. The most authoritative study, released in 2000 by Columbia University law professor James Liebman, found that over two-thirds of U.S. death sentences between 1977 and 1995 were reversed by appellate courts because of error by police, prosecutors, defense counsel, witnesses, or the judiciary.

All in all, these recent trends—public opinion polls and the growing awareness of fundamental inequities and incompetence—suggest that, by and large, Americans are not unreasonable or inhumane. It is reasonable and humane to be concerned about protecting society, about repeat murders, and about the need for compensation of murder victims' families. It is unreasonable, callous, and irresponsible not to deal with these serious problems, and much of the debate has focused on whether the death penalty addresses them effectively and fairly. We have seen much evidence that capital punishment does not resolve these and other issues justly and effectively. We have also been confronted with serious theological questions asking whether capital punishment is consistent with Christian ethics. It is vitally important for death penalty abolitionists and other fair-minded people—Christian and non-Christian alike—to develop public-policy models that give American citizens real alternatives to killing by the state.

State Killing from a Biblical and Christian Perspective

The Hebrew Scriptures

In a pamphlet, *Death as a Penalty*, restorative justice advocate and Mennonite theologian Howard Zehr outlines the role of vengeance and the death penalty in the Old Testament. He makes the following points:

- "An eye for an eye" in the Hebrew Torah was not so much a command to take vengeance as a limit on out-of-proportion family vengeance (Genesis 34:1-29).

- In the Mosaic code, the death penalty was allowed or encouraged for many offenses in addition to murder. Examples include adultery, fornication by an engaged woman, stubborn or rebellious sons, cursing or hitting a parent, working on or defiling the Sabbath, blasphemy, witchcraft, incest, allowing one's dangerous ox to kill, and—ironically—bearing false witness on a capital charge. Thus, those who use the authority of the Old Testament to justify capital punishment today are not consistent unless they also advocate that it be applied across the board to all the offenses cited in the Mosaic code.

- The Old Testament and the later rabbinic tradition placed so many restrictions on the use of the death penalty (Deuteronomy 17, 19) that by the second century it was virtually abolished for most offenses in favor of some form of restitution.

- The story of Cain and Abel (Genesis 4:1-16), the provision of cities of refuge for some killers (Exodus 21, Numbers 35, Deuteronomy 4 and 19, Joshua 20), and the love command in Leviticus 19:18, illustrate the frequent theme of mercy for offenders, even those who kill.

- In the Hebrew Bible, the concept of taking a life for a life functioned more as a sacrificial and ceremonial action than as a legal one (Genesis 9, Exodus 21, Deuteronomy 19).

- The Hebrew concept of justice, in the broader sense, was much more comprehensive than our own, emphasizing *shalom* (peace with justice), or a network of right relationships within a communal context, in which greatly unequal distribution of power and wealth were just as sinful as criminal offenses. Our practice of focusing solely upon the individual criminal offender, and not also on the shared responsibility of the whole community, is much narrower than the biblical perspective, even when we limit ourselves to the Old Testament.

The New Testament

I. *An Experiment:* Read Matthew 27:15-26 and Luke 23:13-31, 39-43. Imagine Jerusalem two thousand years ago. Imagine Jesus called before Pontius Pilate. Pretend that things went a little differently—that Pilate decided to execute Barabbas instead of Jesus. (That is what Pilate had wanted to do before he crumbled under political pressure.) What if he had said, "Okay, Jesus, you can go free on one condition. You must be the executioner of Barabbas. He's a killer, and that's the law. Here's

the hammer. Here are the nails. There's the cross. Go to it."

Can you imagine Jesus hammering those nails into Barabbas's hands and feet? Or, for that matter, flipping the switch on the electric chair, dropping the pellet on cyanide for the gas chamber, or using a hypodermic needle to put Barabbas into a sleep from which he would never awaken. Can you imagine Jesus standing by and allowing someone else to do these things to Barabbas? Could you?

II. *Stone, Cross, Guillotine, Rope, Chair, Needle:* A Meditation on John 8:2-11. Throughout history, civil governments, religious institutions, and lynch mobs have engaged in deliberate, calculated killing of human beings by various methods of execution. Some were "constitutional"; others were no more than intimidation of oppressed groups with "vigilante justice."

If today's lethal injection machine, common in the United States, is the most high-tech way to carry out capital punishment, perhaps stoning, used in biblical times, is the most primitive. There have been times and places in which the death penalty was used to punish only murder. In others, capital crimes ranged from disrespecting your parents to looking at a white woman "funny" if you were black. One biblical scholar found twenty-three capital crimes in the Hebrew Scriptures.

Whatever the method of execution, whatever the crimes punishable by death, whatever the legal or non-legal justification for capital punishment, the common denominator throughout history and across cultures has been this: executioners have always seen themselves as righteous, while the executed have always been seen as the vilest of offenders. Thus, they deserve to be killed, and we deserve to kill them.

Other than Jesus' own execution, capital punishment is rarely mentioned in the Gospels. The most memorable example is found in the story of the woman caught in adultery, a capital crime (John 8:2-11). The scribes and Pharisees are testing Jesus, trying to trick him. It is not clear why only the transgression of the female partner merits stoning to death.

Jesus' response to the authorities' question of whether or not to execute the woman is—typically for him—unexpected, creative, and radical. He completely reframes the issue: "Let anyone among you who is without sin be the first to throw a stone at her" (John 8:7b). The real question is not whether, by law, she deserves to die, but whether the scribes and Pharisees deserve to kill her. As good Jews none of them throw the first stone, for each knows he is not without sin. The only sinless person on the scene, the only one who passes Jesus' own radical test—Jesus himself—chooses not to become an executioner.

Here Jesus is doing the same thing he does in the Sermon on the Mount (Matthew 5-7). He fulfills the law by radicalizing and transforming it. By demanding perfection of his followers and of the would-be executioners, he turns the tables on us all, leaving us to rely solely on his forgiveness and grace rather than on our self-righteousness and idolatry of the letter of the law, constitutional mandates, and due process. Just like the adulterous woman—or the mass murderer on death row—we are still sinners to whom God offers forgiveness.

Is this forgiveness only in the "spiritual realm," leaving us free to continue with our judicial killing in the name of crime control, constitutionality, and due process? Many contemporary Christians think so, but if this dualism had made sense to Jesus, he would have allowed "the authorities" to stone the woman to death while he promised her divine forgiveness. In stopping the execution, he gives us the clear message that God's grace and affirmation of life can extend even to overturning civil law.

In this story Jesus, as always, goes below the surface—deeper than the letter of the law, deeper than the apparent distinction between good people and bad people. He penetrates into the spirit of the law, into the hearts of human beings, and into the very heart of God. He challenges us to go there with him. Two thousand years ago when we executed Jesus we demonstrated that we were afraid to follow him into those depths. Today, at the beginning of a new millennium, a great legal, political, and spiritual struggle over state killing is being fought in our land. Though their pace is beginning to slow, the executions continue. And, in the wake of the September 11, 2001, World Trade Center attack and U.S. military reaction, it appears that the spirit of retribution has once again gained the upper hand. Yet it is never too late for God. Our executed and risen Lord still invites us to put down the stones and move with him into the loving, forgiving, reconciling heart of God.

The United Methodist Church

Since its 1956 General Conference, The Methodist Church and, since 1968, The United Methodist Church have been on record as opposed to capital punishment. This is stated in a clear, forthright manner in the church's Social Principles—between its prohibition of torture and the denunciation of slavery—in the section titled "Basic Freedoms and Human Rights." The church's opposition to state killing is also stated and discussed in several resolutions approved by the 2000 General Conference. In both 2000 and 2001, resolutions calling for the abolition of the death penalty or a moratorium on executions were passed by more annual conferences in the United States than were resolutions on any other issue.

REPARATIONS FOR SLAVERY

by Harmon L. Wray

Whether or not the United States government and/or major U.S.-based corporations owe former slaves and the descendants of slaves some sort of financial restitution or reparation is a question that has been around since the Civil War promise—promptly broken during Reconstruction—of forty acres and a mule for former slaves. Most of the time since then the issue has been on the back burner, but with the turn of the new century it has heated up again. A recent book by scholar-activist Randall Robinson; a run of recent court rulings and settlements; and a series of official government, church, and corporate apologies for past sins of racism and other human rights violations have all resulted in renewed attention to the bill of U.S. Rep. John Conyers, mandating a government study commission on the topic. It is an issue that Conyers has introduced at each session of Congress for several decades. Currently, a team of highly experienced civil rights lawyers are developing strategies for lawsuits concerning various aspects of this complex and multi-faceted issue.

However the matter is eventually resolved, it is in many ways a classic issue of restorative justice, probably not to be raised in a criminal court, though clearly the slave trade and U.S. chattel slavery were crimes against humanity in the profoundest sense. A similar crime was our near-genocide of, and theft of land from, Native Americans (as well as our incarceration of Japanese Americans during World War II). This is a restorative justice issue on a large and historic scale affecting millions of people, as did apartheid in South Africa. Like the global issue of Third World debt, it needs to be addressed from a biblical perspective informed by the Jubilee tradition, the meaning of *shalom*, and the parables of Jesus and his teachings in the Sermon on the Mount. How the ongoing drama surrounding reparations for slavery plays itself out in coming years will be affected by the effectiveness of faith communities and others in the restorative justice movement with which they address the major educational task of insinuating this perspective into the political climate and the public disclosure of U.S. society.

RESOURCES FOR ADDITIONAL INFORMATION

AIM Inc.
P.O. Box 986
Montgomery, AL 36101

Prison PATCH of Chillicothe
(Parents And Their Children)
Box 871
Chillicothe, MO 64601

Prison MATCH of North Carolina
(Mothers And Their Children)
P.O. Box 14469
Raleigh, NC 27620

The Women's Project
222 Main Street
Little Rock, AR 72206

The McCurdy School
P.O. Box 551
Espanola, NM 87532

The Sentencing Project
514 10th Street, NW, Suite 1000
Washington, D.C. 20004
www.sentencingproject.org

National Organization for Victim Assistance (NOVA)
1730 Park Road NW
Washington, D.C. 20010
www.try-nova.org

Website Addresses:

General Board of Global Ministries,
The United Methodist Church
www.gbgm-umc.org

National Center for Elder Abuse (NCEA)
www.gwjapan.com/NCEA

National Institute of Corrections
U.S. Department of Justice
www.ncic.org

Bureau of Justice Statistics
U.S. Justice Department
www.ojp.usdoj.gov/ojs

Brenda Connelly
Brenda ConnellyOAMinistries@aol.com

Marian Styles-McClintock
Deaconesses Cutting Edge Ministries-
Prison Ministries
599 Broadway #3D
Paterson, NJ 07514
973-742-7021
mestel@bellatlantic.net

Harmon L. Wray was executive director of the Restorative Justice Program of the General Board of Global Ministries from January 1999 until October 2001. Previously, Harmon was Coordinator of the Poor and Marginalized for the Tennessee Annual Conference. He has done prison ministry, criminal justice reform, death penalty abolition, and advocacy for victim/offender mediation for almost twenty-six years. Since 1974, he has taught "The Theology and Politics of Crime and Justice in America" at Vanderbilt Divinity School. He is a member of Edgehill United Methodist Church.

A pioneer in restorative justice, Wray helped found the Victim-Offender Reconciliation Program of Nashville, and the Tennessee Coalition to Abolish State Killing. He served as vice-chairperson of the Criminal Justice and Mercy Ministries Networking Group of the Southeastern Jurisdiction of The United Methodist Church.

Wray has written on criminal justice issues, religion and society in the South, and Christian faith in a wide variety of periodicals. He has spoken, taught classes, and conducted workshops on capital punishment, privatization of prisons for profit, the growth of the prison industrial complex, and racism in the criminal justice system.

Peggy Hutchison has been working in the area of restorative justice ministries for over twenty years. As a US-2 person-in-mission in the late 1970s, Hutchison worked with Tucson Metropolitan Ministry on restorative justice ministry issues in Tucson and southern Arizona. In the 1980s, Hutchison coordinated border ministry for the California Pacific and Desert Southwest Annual Conferences. She has served as publisher of a non-governmental educational organization in Washington, D.C. whose mission is to educate North Americans about the contemporary Middle East. In 1995, Hutchison joined the staff of the General Board of Global Ministries as executive secretary for the Middle East and North Africa. In 1996, Hutchison became assistant general secretary for Global Networks and Ecumenical Relations. *(con't)*

Hutchison, convicted (along with eight other sanctuary movement church workers) of conspiracy to violate U.S. laws in 1986, has experienced the injustice of the U.S. criminal justice system. This experience has played a critical role in Hutchison's understanding of restorative justice.

She is married to Michael Elsner, a sociology professor teaching criminology and criminal justice at William Patterson University in New Jersey.

Brenda Connelly is a home missionary of the General Board of Global Ministries serving as a church and community worker. She is the executive director of Older Adult Ministries (OAM), a mission agency of the North Alabama Conference. She works with districts and local churches throughout the conference in developing and implementing ministries in their communities to meet the needs of older adults.

Prior to this assignment, Brenda served as executive director of Robeson County Church and Community Center in Lumberton, North Carolina, in a tri-racial county with high unemployment, adult illiteracy, and substandard housing. She has also served as associate director of Creative Ministries for the Missouri Area United Methodist Churches where she worked primarily with Prison PATCH (Parents And Their Children), a model program for prison inmates and their children.

Brenda is an active member of United Methodist Women and has been a study leader for regional, conference, district, and local mission studies. She and her husband, Richard, are parents of two sons and a daughter.